The Private Club General Manager's Big Game Playbook

Toni Shibayama

Foreword by
Matthew Allnatt
GM/COO, Jonathan Club

D1732778

Dedicated to Brad; my husband and best friend.

Table of Contents

Chapter 1: You've Just Been Named Head Coach 15

Of all the candidates for the head position, it was your vision and ability to guide the team to victory that led to you being chosen. The mission is a simple one; make your Club the ultimate member experience. Are you up to the task?

Chapter 2: Are You Ready for the Season? 21

You landed the job of your dreams. A beautiful facility, loyal employees, dedicated members looking at you to make the best in class Club. Does the staff share *your* vision? Do you have the right people on the team to achieve this vision? How does the staff view your leadership? Have you earned the trust of your team? How will you earn their trust?

Chapter 3: The Need for a Good Coaching Staff.................29

Coaching and leading is a critical role for managers and they need to understand that what they say to others either creates trust or breaks it completely. It just takes one person or government agency to come in to turn everything upside down.

Chapter 4: Does Your Team Need a Salary Cap?

Keep close eyes on your people controlling the financial costs/insurance. These are two critical pieces that all General Managers need to master and focus on. Does the budget drive the mission or the mission drive the budget? What are your financial resources? Do you have a facility with all the bells and whistles, or are you making do with what you have?

Chapter 5: Picking the Team

Landing your new Club is an opportunity to improve weaknesses that have been overlooked in the past. These weaknesses may be the reason you were chosen for the job as it's believed your skill set will fix these. How will you improve the team that is already in place, who very well may be part of these weaknesses?

Chapter 6: The Team Captain Calls the Plays

Who runs the team? It's not the manager, but the people that lead the other employees and have influence over them. Find out who they are and ask them what's working and what's not working. Empower them to keep you informed and keep the culture alive. Ensure their values and priorities align with yours and are broadcast and received on the line.

Chapter 7: Game Day Stress

Undue hardship; anxiety, stress, depression, it all starts with the medical advice and then documentation. Have a wellness plan in place. Train your managers to be sensitive and follow the process. Timing is everything.

How to protect your Club from the big risks and make it a safe haven for members and families. It could be a marquee event gone bad, inappropriate employee behavior, bad press, EPA violations, or simply earning the ire of the surrounding community. Tackle the most important risk that could take your career and Club down for millions of dollars. Don't get knocked out of the game.

We live in a litigious society, so make sure you don't paint a bull-eye on your Club's back by having a shoddy hiring practice or inconsistent workers' comp procedures. Do your due diligence. Be consistent with enforcement. Unhappy employees breed a negative culture and could cost your Club millions in settlements and legal fees.

What happens when the job requires physical tasks but your employee can't do them? This increases the chance of a workers' compensation claim. But could this have been avoided? Management of protected leaves is like walking a tight rope between labor laws and the needs of the operations. You get hit with lawsuits, government fines, fraudulent workers' comp claims, audits, and all of a sudden your risk factors have doubled, resulting in enormous and crippling costs.

Your Club needs to be "protected" by an internal skilled HR professional, outside local labor attorney, industry specific insurance broker and a veteran risk manager. And they all need to be consulted for their expert advice before pulling the trigger and opening up a Pandora's Box of complex and stressful liability that could impact the Club for years to come.

Look to your veteran players and don't shy away from expectations and succession planning. Education is the key to preparing and planning for retirement. Remember the three critical pieces of the pie; Social Security, Medicare and a Retirement Program.

The accolades come flowing in. You're the best General Manager and COO in the industry; but did this happen overnight? Of course not; it took vision, dedication, and commitment. You've created the Club version of the New England Patriots and Pittsburgh Steelers and forged a dynasty. Congratulations!

FOREWORD

Go on to the Amazon website and search "How-To Books." I guarantee you'll come across thousands of them. How-to-do this and how-to-do that. And most of them not worth the paper they're printed on. But if you dig deep you'll uncover a gem or two; a how-to-do book that actually *shows you how-to-do something*. That's the book that can change your professional life, can help you do your job more efficiently, and can make your vision the vision of others. It's simply because the author knew the right words to get that message across.

With 20-plus years working with some of the top Private Clubs in the country, I'm happy to say; Toni Shibayama knows the right words.

I've known Toni for over 20 years, having first worked with her when I was the GM at Wilshire Country Club in Los Angeles, California. At that time she was helping us with our HR and performing risk management duties. And what struck me right off the bat was how hard she worked. She's always available and her attention to detail was magnificent. This was a tremendous help to me back then because I couldn't really afford a full-blown HR Department. Human Resources back then was very different than it is today. It was extremely complicated and I knew I needed an experienced partner. And even though back then Toni's company was small, she had a lot of energy. She protected me from lawsuits and helped me become compliant. From there the relationship just grew as Toni started to think of other things she could do for us.

One of the things I learned very early on in my career was you hire to fill an area you're weak in. It's very hard to look somebody in the eye and say, "I really love HR. It keeps me up at night with excitement." When the truth is all the time you're worrying about lawsuits and training and workers' compensation and a dozen other things. But Toni actually gets excited about such things, and she comes to the table prepared. And if there is something she can't do she will say so; then go and figure out how to do it.

So, does this make Toni qualified to write a playbook that every new GM should read as they begin their new adventure? Very much so. Like red wine certain things get better with age, and working with GMs for more than two decades she has seen the right thing to do and the wrong thing to do. She has worldly experience and that's extremely important. I would say that

Toni Shibayama has basically seen and done everything. She has watched me and other GM's make an unbelievable amount of mistakes. And she cares so much that when she sees these mistakes being made she promises that will never happen to another GM.

If Toni's book emphasizes anything it's that we are in the people business. And that is the piece that makes our job really difficult. But you've got to accept that's the reason you got into this business in the first place. Someone once said, "This job would be really easy if I didn't work for people, and I didn't have people working for me." But it is what it is, and human beings are very complicated people. And, you can never tell what they're going to do, what they're going to say. All you can do is your very best to stay ahead of it. And I think for a new GM, you can never know enough.

When you come into a Club there are a bunch of other things going on, and HR is low on the list of priorities. But when you read this book you'll realize that shouldn't be the case because there are so many different scenarios being played out that can impact your Club, and not for the better. Fortunately, Toni has trained and mentored lots of new GMs, and made them realize they *are* in the people business.

One of the key sections of this book is the need to properly and honestly evaluate your current team. But it's not the golf pro or the chef or the line employees that will be the potential issue; it's going to be your management team. If you're brought in to be successful, then you're likely brought in to change a culture that starts from the top. And the biggest mistake most new GMs make, myself included, is being afraid to make that tough decision. And Toni's strength is in helping GMs navigate smoothly through that process because it also can be insanely disruptive because those tough decisions often affect people who have allies among employees and among the members. When there are rough seas ahead, you want Toni steering the ship.

The title of this book is *The Private Club General Manager's Big Game Playbook*. It's not *The NEW Private Club General Manager's Big Game Playbook*. This means that even existing General Managers can find value in what Toni has to say, if for no other reason than the world is constantly shifting beneath our feet, with new regulations, new laws, and more categories of protected leaves than you can shake a stick at. To be caught off guard is to put your Club at risk.

It's very apropos that Toni model her book after sports, because I think the most important job of a GM is to be a coach. You're not the golf pro, you're not the CFO, you're not the HR Director, you're not the Head Chef, *but you do need to give them the game plan.* And so using some of the tools that Toni provides to motivate and to excite, to bring the team together, is critical. I've always said that as a General Manager my job is to know what sort of talent I have on my team and then give them the game plan to run with.

That's what this book is all about. *How to do it.*

Matthew Allnatt, GM & COO
Jonathan Club
Santa Monica, CA

INTRODUCTION

Do what you love.

We've all heard that mantra before, but it's rarely something that is put into practice. What I do as a Risk Manager is not work; it's a passion. I was lucky enough to join my father's firm and had the opportunity to be part of a team that serviced an exclusive high-end country club. That Club was Riviera Country Club. It had a rich history and an iconic golf course, but it was the staff that I fell in love with.

Walking into the Club I saw many friends and you could feel the emotional connection to kind and warm individuals that truly cared about the Club. I knew then I wanted to help others in the industry; learn about their fears, protect them from risks, and to help them focus on their bottom line. However, you can't do that without wanting to know the ins and outs of the industry. My childlike curiosity has allowed me to see first-hand successes and turbulent failures, and how not to repeat them.

Working for so many years in the industry, I have uncovered one undisputable fact; team members embody hospitality. They love their job with all their heart because it is effortless and fun.

They create moments of joy (recreation, holidays, weddings, wine tastings, competitive games of pickleball, etc.). Could there be a better job? So why does it seem so difficult for some Clubs and so easy for others?

In my nearly 25 years of experience in the Club industry, I've witnessed amazing triumphs and a formula for success. While some of the chapters in this book may not be a revelation, it is my hope that they will still serve as a savvy reminder and a cautionary tale to be learned from others.

What you read will encompass The Three P's:

People: Do you have the right players to make a winning team? Hiring, retirement, injuries, coaches, etc.

Process/Protection: Are you up to speed on training, practicing, and coaching while identifying your risk and putting in proper prevention and building your trusted protection team?

Promote: The lifeblood of a Club is membership. If you have a superior Club, let the world know. Shout it to the mountain tops. Why not? You're the best.

Question: Do your employees believe, feel and see this as ONE team and ONE vision. Is this *their* mantra?

We are the best Club

We have the best facilities

We have world class amenities

We have an impeccable staff dedicated to service

We are the Club of choice and we have a robust membership waiting list

All future generations will want to be part of the Club

It's your job to take your Club to the next level. You have the talent, skill and the tools to do it. You have the right players; now be the best Head Coach you can be.

Let the games begin!

Toni Shibayama

CHAPTER 1

You've Just Been Named Head Coach

"Your TALENT determines what you can do. Your MOTIVATION determines how much you are willing to do. Your ATTITUDE determines how well you do it." - Lou Holtz

You've just been informed that you landed a new position at that Private Club you've had your sights on for years. At this point it's normal to be overwhelmed with a flurry of emotions; excitement, apprehension, and trepidation. Perhaps you even start doubting yourself with questions like; "Can I deliver what I promised?" and "What is expected of me?"

Perhaps some of these questions are being stimulated by making the advancement from a mid-level Club to a high-end operation. So you are asking yourself; "Am I ready to take that next step?" Perhaps at your prior Club you oversaw a $1 million Club renovation. Now you'll have a $25 million Club renovation. But don't be intimidated by the numbers. You've been through the golf course renovation scenario before. Trust me, they all have the same things in common; grass and holes. Think of it this way; if you can successfully paint a split-level ranch house, then you can paint a three-level colonial. It's the same concept; just bigger so you have to buy more paint.

I would also counter those doubts by saying this is an exciting opportunity and the next level in your career. You got to this point due to your expertise, your knowledge base, and a belief that you can inspire your team to move to that next level. You most likely already have that raw talent in place, and they may just need somebody to identify the talent, to coach the talent, encourage the talent and motivate that talent to get to that next level. After all, you are the newly-named coach for a team with the aspiration of getting to the Super Bowl.

Still, it's only natural to have some doubts. Is everyone going to love me? Will they follow me into battle? But you have to remember that your team has those same fears; is the new coach going to like me or fire me? Will I be put in a position to advance and succeed, or should I update my resume? Yes, you have your work cut out for you because you were hired over possibly hundreds of candidates because those making the decision were sold on your ability to implement your vision to attain their vision, which is to make your Club the ultimate member experience. You are the new super-hero on the block, and like Spiderman, with great power comes great responsibility.

When hired you were told the goal is to be the number one local Club. They that they want to have the best member experience. But what does that really mean? In order for you to know that, you need to know what are the benchmarks that you're going to have to reach to achieve whatever lofty goals have been placed in front of you. But before you can achieve those benchmarks you have to first ascertain if your new employer is making the transition into your new role as smooth as possible, so you can hit the ground running. And this means even before you meet that first member of your staff.

What is your first day on the job going to look like? Are you going to be greeted by people? Is your desk put together? Is your email set up? Do you have a set of keys? Have you been given a walk through? Did they put a plant in your new office? Do you have business cards? Is your phone set up? Did they clean up your office? Or was nothing done because everybody was taking vacations and you were pretty much an afterthought? So, what does that tell you coming in? And what was your first impression of the Club?

These are going to be little indicators of process, procedure and getting things done because if the Club can't do the simple things for a new general manager, how are they going to successfully service their members? It's like they gave you the keys to the kingdom and then changed the locks.

Once you finally figure out where the restrooms are, a new GM needs to set a level of expectation, both for himself/herself and for the members. You have to understand what an amazing member experience looks like in order to determine how close you are to achieving it. On a scale of one to 10, are you a nine and well on your way to excellence? Or are you a one and really have your work cut out for you? How do we know where you rank? Do you look at membership surveys in regards to food, cleanliness, and those types of things? If one of the answers to your survey is simply, "I want better customer service." What does that mean? Can you give an example?

The bottom-line is you were hired for your vision, but how do you know your vision is attainable? I have seen some gung-ho GMs go in with unattainable visions. And when they realize they can't reach those lofty goals it all falls to pieces. So, ask yourself: are they realistic goals? Because there are realistic visions and unrealistic visions. You can tell the people making the hiring decision everything you want, but it doesn't mean you can do it. Did you set realistic goals?

I think a lot of times people believe they can succeed with their vision by just having more money to work with. But not everything can be fixed with money. What needs to be in place are benchmarks that you can achieve, even before you start sitting down and talking with your managers. Then, when you do meet for the first time with your staff, you will be able to determine if they are up for the challenge. At that point you will know if certain things are attainable. You certainly don't want to walk in and fire everybody and start from scratch. So you will need managers that are willing to be *honest* and say, "Here's my crew. I've got two rookies. I've got a couple of new managers that I'm training who are working out pretty well. And I've got two people out on disability, although one just posted a photo of himself on social media bouncing on a backyard trampoline."

Once you know what the key benchmarks are, and how to achieve them, any doubt or trepidation will seep away. Only then will you be able to take charge of your team and accomplish the mission at hand. After all, you've trained all your life for this move. Sure, there will be more eyes on you and higher expectations, like moving up from a minor league park to a full-blown stadium. And those fans will be more rabid and more focused on winning because they are paying a lot more money for their game-day tickets. But you are up for the task; bring it on.

Now, let's go meet your team.

Action Points:

- Establish the vision for the Club
- Establish goals to make the vision a reality
- Establish benchmarks and timelines on deliverables to achieve the goals

A Final Thought:

"Excellence is not a spectator sport. Everyone's involved."
—Jack Welch

CHAPTER 2

Are You Ready for the Season?

"WINNING is not everything. But making the EFFORT to win is"- Vince Lombardi

You've landed your dream job. Now what?

For most people, when they take over a top position the first thing that goes through their minds is, "What am I inheriting for staff?" And that question is usually followed by three different responses.

Some will keep the status quo; if it's not broke, why fix it? Some will do a surgical strike and weed out several top positions either because they have someone else in mind, or they simply want to make a change for the sake of change. And then there are those who will immediately think the best course of action is to start with a clean slate; to carpet bomb the entire staff. Sadly, all three techniques are a recipe for disaster.

The first thing new GM's need to do is take the emotion out of whatever it is they are thinking of doing, before they even step through the door on that first day. Because now's the time to do a 90-day assessment of the staff. And that starts with a SWOT exercise.

SWOT stands for Strength, Weaknesses, Opportunities, and Threats. And all four of these factors, either individually or collectively, can create a roadmap to whether your Club *can* and *will* be successful.

It's you saying here are our **strengths** and what we do well, so let's keep it up because this is what makes us who we are. We're the leader; the purple cow. There may still some **weaknesses** in our game, perhaps in regards to service, consistency, the quality of the food, member relations, the facilities, and other items that do not meet and exceed member expectations. As for **opportunities**, are we missing the boat? Could we bring in more junior memberships? Could we be expanding the overall membership, or a different layer of membership? How about tournaments, events? Are we ready to deal with **threats**, which could be anything from a new Club opening up next door to us, the economy tanking and people not having that discretionary income, any sort of government regulation—a pandemic?

Think of it as training camp prior to the start of the season. It's about being observant and taking it all in, not jumping to conclusions, and not emotionally trying to change things. It's about seeing who you have, who's your team, who are your mid-level managers; take a pulse. Are people happy? Are they satisfied with their current pay? Do they understand the vision and the core values of the Club? You should sit down with each of the employees and ask them, "What are we doing right and what are we doing wrong? Do you feel comfortable? Do you feel safe? Do you feel that we're being honest with you?" It gives an opportunity for that one on one connection, because sometimes you're viewed as being high a top of the castle and totally inaccessible. This is really an opportunity to get to know everybody because you will only be successful if they are.

Nobody likes change, and it's a very fearful time. People feel like they are being re-interviewed for their job. But you don't have to be the Grim Reaper. It's just really identifying their strengths and weaknesses and putting together the best team. Ask the important questions; "Why are you part of the Club? Why have you been here for 20 years? What makes us special? Tell us a few things that are special about the Club." Those seemingly innocuous answers will pave the way to becoming a successful Club.

Gregg Patterson worked for 30-plus years at one of the most successful Clubs in Santa Monica, and he was beloved by his staff. He said this dedication was because he made it a point of knowing one thing about every one of his employees. He says, "My employees take care of some of the richest people in the world, right? And they deal with our members with a smile, and they give them great service; kind of like a family. But I can only gain their trust if they know that I care about them, I greet them, I talk to them, and I treat my hourly workers the same way I would a billionaire."

That connection is extremely important in regards to knowing what you're getting yourself into. Who do you have as far as employees? Sadly, a lot of new GMs go in with the preconceived idea that they want to make changes, and that's when bad things can happen.

That being said, it would be naïve to think that some people will not resent the new person coming in. Maybe they were good friends with the outgoing person and they have a hidden agenda. What are the warning signs? Perhaps during a staff meeting you get a lot of less-than-sincere nods from a particular person. Maybe he's doodling while you are speaking. Maybe even the occasional eyeroll while you're outlining your vision for the future. You can tell right away that this person hasn't bought in, and it would be a simple task at that point to pull out the axe and chop away. But should you?

Nobody likes change, or at the very least it invites pushback. But instead of setting a bad example in front of the troops by playing public executioner, which can only instill negative collateral damage, the path of least resistance might be to try and bring them into the fold. Explain to them that you have observed there may be some objection to some things you've outlined. How can we get on the same page? Let them know you *want* them on the same page, that you want their input. People want to feel wanted (and people, who need people, are the luckiest people in the world).

When I talk to GMs, I always challenge them to find out good things about the ones they've categorized as "bad apples." Are they beloved by their co-workers and membership? Are they part of the culture? Are they friends with all the board members that actually hired you? Do they know where the bodies are buried? Do they know the fabric of the community here and, therefore, should you keep them versus a knee jerk reaction? But in doing so, will you create a toxic environment that will sabotage everything you're trying to do?

Perhaps the best way to avoid putting yourself in that precarious position is to keep it from happening in the first place. So, how do you do this?

The first thing to do is line up your superstars; separate the plow horses from the race horses, but never lose fact that both are important. It's all about assessing your talent, because your most important asset is your people. I recently worked with a particular GM, and he's great guy. He's a tough East Coast guy with a dry sense of humor, but lovable. He's tough, but if you do a good job, he's the first one to get on the stage and give you applause. He holds these all-staff meetings and people are raising their hands because he's asking everyone a question about themselves, like "What good thing have you done for a member recently?" And then someone mentions they had a member who had a flat tire and no AAA, so they went out and changed his tire. People are applauding this like someone just won an Oscar. Everybody is buying into this. And then he invites in the board members and all the employees applaud them for keeping the Club successful and paying for their wages and being a member. It's a love-fest. They get it, and they want to see their peers succeed. *They want the Club to succeed*. It's a true Kumbaya moment.

You need to remember that you have not just been named the GM of Cheesecake Factory or Home Depot, where you may not see the same customer twice. As is the case with private membership, Clubs have a set number of people that are coming and going. You, and your staff, have the advantage of familiarity; what does that member like at the bar, what's his favorite tee time, and when's his wife's birthday? And this familiarity is rooted in the idea that change for the sake of change is a bad thing, one that could result in a huge disaster that can turn a ripple effect into a tsunami of bad feelings.

If you're looking to make change, make it positive change, the kind that you can actually quantify and visualize to everybody else. Ask somebody who's been in the same position for 20 years if they would like to be in another position. Do they have any aspirations? Maybe they want to be a souse chef. We do a disservice if we don't encourage training and advancements within. Some of the most successful GMs all worked their way up. Maybe they started as a short order cook and a GM saw something in them. They saw the vision. It's like, "I remember Maria when she was in housekeeping and now she's head the entire department." I think that it's really important to identify some diamonds in the rough, really diehard employees who are itching and looking for that opportunity.

And once you accomplished all this, once you've successfully completed that 90-day training camp, then you're ready to start the season.

Action Points:

- 90-day team member / department assessment
- Strengths/Weaknesses/Opportunities/Threats analysis
- Schedule your individual team member meetings

A Final Thought:

"True leadership is the art of changing a group from what it is into what it ought to be. It's not something that is done "to" people, it is something done "with" people. By that definition, every person on the team is a leader." - Jan Greene

CHAPTER 3

The Need for a Good Coaching Staff

"Coaching is not how much you KNOW. It's how much you can get players to DO."- Bum Phillips

The winningest Head Coaches in the NFL—Don Shula, George Halas, Bill Belichick, Tom Landry—did not achieve this lofty status in a vacuum. They were hoisted to these rarified heights on the shoulders of their Assistant Coaches, the individuals who were at all times in direct contact with the troops on the field; the Offensive Coach, Defensive Coach, Lineman Coach, Special Teams Coach, and so forth.

Put in the lexicon of Private Clubs, these would be your Club managers, the folks heading up various departments who must be laser-focused to keep your members happy, your board content, and your business successful. They are your day-to-day managers; your department heads, all tasked with a critical mission and all of equal importance. Your Club is a chain and these are your links. If one breaks, so will the integrity of what you are trying to hold together. And as the newly-arrived GM, it's imperative that you know everything about them and what they believe. Here is your triumvirate:

Director of Golf

This is the person facilitates golf and not only encourage the game but enhances it and is in charge of the golf pros, the bag room, the starters, and the Pro Shop.

Grounds Superintendant

This is the person in charge of the grounds, the individual who makes the difference whether you have a pristine five-star course or a big grassy field with a bunch of holes in it. He/she knows the science—the special sauce—to make the course the best it can be. He/she has the largest staff and if you don't see him/her and his/her crew out on the course by 5:00am, mowing the grass and tending the bunkers, chances are they overslept. It's all science and stuff like that. They're usually one of your highest paid managers and worth it for obvious reasons.

Director of Food & Beverage

They oversee the kitchen staff, wait staff, catering, etc. They interface during regular dining experiences and make holidays and events special and memorable. It's a high stress and fast moving department with many different personalities maintaining a cool and courteous demeanor.

From there the coaching levels filter down to the CFO, Human Resources, Membership Director, Marketing, Communications, Catering Director, Head Chef, Engineers, Purchasing and Administration Team. All of the various departments work together as one.

It's important to note that not all departments are invited to the "High Table," so if the mandates being discussed at the leadership meeting get lost in translation when moving down a rung on the corporate ladder to these departments, then there is a good chance the train will go off the tracks.

Your top Assistant Coaches need to be an extension of you and willing to pass down your message as succinctly as possible. If you say, "We've got to go down this path and then in this direction," the leaders need to then regurgitate that to their teams and not just say to them, "Hey, you're all on board, right?" Your Assistant Coaches are the catalyst to get things done, so they have to believe it as well. Every new GM has to create that little circle of trust, so they know that their leadership team is going back to their respective departments and communicating what we are doing as a team. The GM can't say something to the Director of Food & Beverage, and then have him/her go rogue and tell the kitchen staff something different. And when I see people doing this pushing back, it's because they're not giving the full reason as to why this new GM thinks his idea is a good one.

Speaking in tongues will never work—it's not your department head's job to try and interpret what you are saying (and if they can't understand it, how can they properly translate it to their staff.) Be concise and uber-clear in the message you want passed on. After all, the message Paul Revere was asked to pass on was simply *"The British are coming!"* Think of what shape our country would be in today if that message was, *"It has come to our attention, through scientific data gathered at various interludes, and subject to clarification and best practices put on by years of study, and subject to analysis of 10-20% variables, that, it appears, the British are coming."* We'd all be playing soccer instead of football.

As the new Head Coach, you also have to be wary of any bad vibrations being given off by your leadership team as you sit at the High Table with your new band of Merry Men (and women). You need to be able to tell, hopefully as soon as possible, who might not be onboard or disengaged. It could be someone who has been there for 20-plus years and is checking his phone calendar everyday to see when he can retire. It could be that perhaps one of the team thought they should be sitting at the head of the table. And it could also be as simple as someone just not liking change. That vibration could be subtle, no more than a small murmur. But it could also be the equivalent of a jet taking off. Either way, you need to watch for it and address it, sooner rather than later. If you notice someone totally disengaged, take them aside after the meeting and ask them if there was something in the plan they felt uncomfortable about, and if so what would be their suggestion? The goal: stop them before they pass along the wrong information.

A good GM will sniff out somebody who's not on board pretty quickly. Either they're pushing back or they're not delivering. They're not communicating with their team. And to that end I would say that it's really important for the GM to ask the people that are in place what's working and what's not working; get their feedback. You have to build their trust, or they can't help you do your job.

So how many members of your leadership team are potential push backers, for lack of a better phrase? How many are potential problems? My experience, it's probably half, and here's why. If they've seen a lot of turnover, they are likely thinking, "I'll probably outlast this new person, so how much time and energy should I invest in what he has to say." But if you don't have a collaborative idea of vision and a plan that you create *with* your leadership team, there's more chance of them pushing back because they don't have any ownership, they have no feedback in it, and no dog in the fight. And if they've been doing their job for 10 years and you just come in and you're telling them how to do their job, a job they have done successfully for a decade or more, then you're more likely to see push back versus collaboration. The blowback will be, "I've been doing it this way forever. Why change?" You have to make them buy into your vision by making them feel like it is a shared vision (even if it's not). Otherwise you are trying to get that ball over the goal line from the two yard line with no blockers and the entire L.A. Rams defensive line standing in your way. And this is where your 90-day assessment and SWOT analysis exercise is so key.

Earning the trust of your coaching stuff begins by getting them to help craft the plan because they're going to have to be doing the heavy lifting. Map out the goals and deadlines; make it a project. And in doing so you'll get more of a buy-in instead of having people pushing back. Sometimes you need to devote a little more time and attention to those that need to be on your side. Because, ultimately, if they're not following you, then they're turning people against you.

But remember, no Super Bowl was ever won without ruffling some feathers, so make sure you are okay with that. Although it may seem that way at first, there are no sacred cows. A successful GM can't work from a position of weakness because if they do, then they become pretty much chum in the waters and the predators will circle quickly. They can smell... *apprehension.*

Here's another way to think of it. If you're a teacher and you have 80% of the class that's onboard and following the syllabus and getting a B-grade or above, chances are you'll be spending less time with them because they are on track. It's the 20% that you have to pull a little bit closer and try to understand the reasons why they "don't get it." Is it because they can't or don't want to get it, or do they fail to get it because the lesson being taught isn't clear to them?

Every new GM should be looking at the SWOT analysis of their coaches, do they need coaching for their coaching skills? Are they able to lead a team? Do they have the emotional intelligence training? Do they think that just because they have the credentials and they've been in a job for a long time, that they have the respect and trust from their employees? Maybe they don't. It's your job to help them find the motivation to gain that trust and respect. Because what good is it, after you've worked so hard to get your leadership team to buy in to your message, if their employees are ignoring it when if filters down from someone they don't respect?

It's also important that the new GM keep a watchful eye on potential areas of risk, especially as it pertains to his coaching staff, since they are the ones in the trenches day in and day out. Let's say we have to deal with a fraudulent workers' comp claim or a lawsuit at some point and we finally have to fire somebody. I always have the GM ask the manager, "Was this a surprise? Did you know before this that they were a horrible employee for 20 years?" If they say yes, the next question is, "Then why didn't you do something about it?" It's your manager's job to know where the weaknesses are and where the most risk lurks.

Let's take it by department. The Director of Golf always needs to have hospitality in mind because for the most part he/she works directly with the members and their needs.

He/she's working with skilled people, like the golf pros, who are in direct contact with your members, so their mandate is, "How can I make your experience enjoyable here and sociable at the Club?" Risk can ensue when perhaps the pro interprets social behavior as an off-color joke, or an inappropriate touch. The Director of Golf also oversees the pro shop, making sure it looks nice and has the most up-to-date equipment. And you're dealing with hundreds and thousands of dollars of equipment as well, so you want to make sure you have a pretty good handle on inventory, especially as it pertains to employee theft. Along the same lines, members are always leaving their bags around, often with money in them, so you need to make sure these bags are stored properly and the people storing them are fully vetted. Same situation with the locker rooms.

The Grounds Superintendent falls into a whole other category of risk. Along with workers falling into the obvious category of workers' comp—tumbling off ladders and trucks, being on the wrong wide of a hedge clipper—this person lives in a dangerous world of combustible chemicals and highly-flammable solutions. Add in all the pesticides needed to prevent your golf course from becoming a giant insect buffet, and you can see the risks immediately. Safety here has to be the number-one priority.

It doesn't take a rocket scientist to know where the risks lurk for the Director of Food & Beverage. Somebody cooks bad food and it goes through the Club like wildfire. And anyone who has ever been in a busy kitchen knows it is a pretty dangerous place; knives are sharp, pans are hot, floors are slippery. Plus, there's also the added element of a ticking clock. In the time it might take you or I to read through a cookbook to even *find* a 6-course meal to prepare, the Head Chef and his staff are already plating. Accidents can, and will, happen. The kitchen is a risk magnet. There can also be risks in the bartending area. By the very nature of the business there occurs a level of camaraderie between member and bartender that always teeters on the prospect of risk. And, again, all it takes is an off-handed comment or an off-color joke to push it over the edge. They think that because a member is joking around it's okay and that's part of the job. I tend to see those things blow up because sometimes people don't know where that line is drawn.

When you venture into what the CFO and HR deal with you're talking cyber attacks, theft, embezzlement, plus wage and hour disputes with employees, all the fun things in the world. These are the risks that your leadership team faces every day. And it's your job, as the GM, to know who is watching for what, before it reaches a critical level and finds its way back to you. You don't want to be last man standing.

Keep an eye on your top areas of risk. It can take just one person or government agency to come in to turn everything upside down. Make strategic business decisions and verify with checklists for best practices and to minimize collateral damage that can trail you for years to come. That one person could be bringing a class action lawsuit for sexual harassment, while a government agency could be OSHA coming in with a significant fine, or another agency conducting a wage and hour audit that could take you down as well.

It's usually an afterthought, but if you don't train your managers to be leaders, and teach them how to be on the lookout for potential risk, you will see high turnover lawsuits and workers' comp fraud. You need to make sure your leadership team has a true understanding of how to coach their staff, how to delicately train them and give them encouragement, and how to know when to talk to them. People need to get better, and you can only do that by bringing things to their attention. In general, most issues happen because things are left unsaid. When things are not approached in a timely manner they will fester. It's often a tough role to manage people, to coach them, to lead them. But it's very likely that is why you were chosen to be the Head Coach. And if you have any aspirations to being among the winningest Head Coaches, then it's your leadership team—your Assistant Coaches—that are going to hoist you above the rest.

Action Points:

- Collaborate with your Department Heads to establish goals

- Assess the needs of your Department Heads

- Provide your Department Heads with the skills and training they need and want

A Final Thought:

"The job of the leader is not to kick people in the butt; it's to mobilize them to take action." - Unknown

CHAPTER 4

Does Your Team Need a Salary Cap?

"We would ACCOMPLISH many more things if we did not think of them as IMPOSSIBLE."- Vince Lombardi

When any new GM takes over the team, there are two important areas to focus on; staff and budget. Does the budget drive the mission or the mission drive the budget? And does the budget identify the objective as a result of strategic planning process and the alignment of short and intermediate goals?

Is the new GM's vision in line with the Club's? Does the Club want to be the next Pebble Beach and attract those types of members, or are they okay being a level two golf course? This is perhaps where the budget is driving the mission. The money's coming in from membership, and if you have a really low number of members and you don't charge them enough, and your expectations are you're going to be the Ritz Carlton, then you're just never going to be able to make those leaps and bounds. You have to make sure that the goals and objectives that you have to meet are financial goals as well.

Maybe you want to have the world's best golf course, but that's going to cost $20 million and you have only $5 million to play with. That's when your expectations exceed your budget. You have to make sure those expectations are realistic and sustainable; you don't want to redo your clubhouse, or your greens or your golf course every year. You want them to be long lasting because you don't want to have to keep going back to your members and assessing them another $100 for their rest of their life, versus it being within the operating budget. And if the members say, "I don't want to be charged." Then you have to set levels on those expectations. You don't want to be the Club that's charging big bucks but still presenting as a level two Club.

But once you become that Big Bucks Club, expectations grow exponentially. Let's take for example a Club which sits on the most expensive land in town. They spend big money on their golf courses and their services. The member's mentality is they live in one of the richest parts of the world, they vacation in Bali, stay at five-star hotels, and when they come to this Club, which they pay a lot of money for, if the dinner order is incorrect or the service is slow, they're thinking all this money is going somewhere and maybe somebody is pocketing it. That member's expectations are not being filled. Members want—and need—to see where their money is going.

If you are spending $375,000 for a Club membership, what does that $375,000 look like? If you're spending $65,000, you might have some brown patches. You're likely going to have an old antiquated ballroom. Your locker room is going to be just so-so and the women's locker room is going to be maybe two closets. So, what do you do to attract new members, knowing you are perhaps already pushing the envelope on membership fees versus the features being offered? You make the decision to be family friendly and you put in a bocce ball course and a swimming pool and upgrade your gym facility. You make your Club family friendly because you want your members to think of it as their home away from home. It's more value for their membership dollar. But that investment still needs to make sure it aligns with where the Club is going. And do you have the budget for these changes? If you don't have the budget for it, and you need $10 million or $15 million more, are you okay moving forward with raising membership fees. And if you raise those fees, have you also concurrently raised your member's expectations? And, most importantly, have you satisfied those new expectations?

What if, as the new GM coming in, you ask the superintendent who is in charge of the golf course about his $3 million budget and what his business plan is, only to have him reply, "We don't really have a business plan, the $3 million is for payroll." To which you reply, "But you know where every dollar is going, right?" You're keeping an eye on increases in wages because of the minimum wage coming up. And you know if we have a lot of accidents that our workers' comp may double as well and it will be hitting our operating budget?" This is about the time the superintendant remembers an important phone call he has to make. The problem is that unless your operating budget is tied into a business plan it's like money blowing in the wind; you're never going to get a handle on it.

Is the business plan/operating budget sustainable? Because, as sure as death and taxes, everything is going up. Salaries are number one, followed closely by insurance. If a Club doesn't manage its insurance it could be looking at an extra $300-$400,000 per year. Then what happens if that GM has to tell the board they have to raise membership fees to cover the costs and suddenly you have 600 members saying, "What the hell is going? Are you not running this Club correctly?" So you have to keep an eye on things to make sure you are operating within that budget and then forecasting whether there's going to be impacts to payroll and insurance. You have to make sure each department knows where their budget is going.

So, how do these departments budget against unknown variables? It could be a typhoon or it could be a pandemic. What if something happens beyond your control? Do you have a rainy-day fund? The problem is that most people think insurance is going to cover whatever comes down the road, but that virus that just shut down your Club isn't covered by insurance.

But let's circle back to the vision. The board and the GM most likely have come together as far as what the vision is, and that usually involves either a change in management or a change to the facility. If you're talking facility-wise, then it's millions of dollars for a new clubhouse, new golf course, you name it. The other part of it is your team, which means you can either train for excellence or you can buy excellence. You have to look at who you have and if they are they living up to that level of standard you've established for your Club. If you want high quality talent, either you train who you have, or you have to pay top dollar to bring in a new person. Can you teach your backup quarterback to be a winner, or are you going to have to pay big bucks in free agency to bring in Tom Brady? Will your budget work with who you have, or do you have to go to a recruiter to bring in fresh blood?

Another problem we have seen is the Clubs that don't have expensive membership fees yet are building way above member expectations. And that can only lead to financial trouble. There's a Club in South Pasadena, in an area that was very swanky in the 1950s and 1960s. But over time, the demographics and also the median home and salary went down drastically. Now they're competing with a gorgeous Club not too far away and they are going after the same high-end members. As a result, the pool is shrinking, which is bad for both Clubs, but perhaps more for the Club that builds a gorgeous facility but doesn't have the membership to support them long-term. Because at the end of the day it's all about finding out what the vision of the club is long-term, what their mission is, and does that mission live in reality. And do you have the long-term membership to sustain such a Club?

When it comes to revenue streams, memberships are the blood of the Club, in fact it's everything. And it can be multigenerational where you have a member forever and their kids and family. It's where you are told don't look at that

46

member as Mr. Johnson; look at him like he's a million dollars. Because that's how much he's going to spend. Other than that, it's going to be income from events. The CFOs get excited about events because for them it is like found money. And if you're located in a place like Southern California sometimes studios will do a buyout for your location for shooting a TV show or a commercial. But everything really is about getting membership and that membership needs to be a good fit. Because if they're happy they're going to be with you for a very long time. And that helps because being attached to a cool Club makes them cool, and who doesn't want to hang around with cool people, which can increase your membership. You don't want a member for a year; you want a member forever. You want that member to be perpetual. Like a timeshare. That is the Club that will continue to thrive.

The flip side of the coin is the Club that is obviously not cool. They are running two-for-one specials asking you to bring a guest in with you. That guest plays a round of golf, chows down at the clubhouse, maybe gets drunk, and then vanishes forever. So, what you just did was water down your membership, which is a disservice both to you and the other members who call the Club their home. Not cool.

Country clubs are all quite different, and I would say for the most part they don't usually compete with each other. If you're uber-wealthy, you just belong to all of them. They usually all keep a set of golf clubs at each place too. They like the feeling of belonging; like their little Oasis away from home and business.

Finally, an incoming GM has to always be aware of a change in demographics, whereas it's the demographics that drive the membership fees and the subsequent budget. And interestingly enough, as much as the recent pandemic brought business to a halt, it has also led to resurgence in the popularity of golf because it's one of the safest sports because it's played outdoors and you're social distancing. Thus, we're seeing the natural progression of more families. This means Clubs can now be a little more casual, whereas before you would get dirty looks if you wore jeans. And I think people are saying, if we stick with that old model, we will crumble and die.

You need to keep a balance between new members and old members. If you need to undertake a complete redo of the golf course and it's going to be $40,000 for every member, the older members aren't going to be happy about shutting down the course for two years because they feel they only have so many of those years left. On the other hand, the younger members will think it's great because they will have a better course. Time is on their side.

There's always going to be that push back of the old and new, but you have to look at it as, "Is it good for the long-term?" There is usually a divide between older members because of their niche and newer members who are looking at it more of an investment long-term and maybe for their kids as well. And that is a good thing because as we have alluded to previously, the goal should be to set a budget based on sustainability, and work within that budget, but never lose sight of the vision.

Action Points:

- Review the operation budget
- The vision needs to be supported by the budget
- Envision the future and the budget that is needed

A Final Thought:

"Courage is what it takes to stand up and speak; courage is also what it takes to sit down and listen." - Winston Churchill

CHAPTER 5

Picking the Team

"How do you win? By getting average players to play good and good players to play great. That's how you win."
- Bum Phillips

It's been said that a chain is only as strong as its weakest link, and that pretty much sums up what often awaits a new GM. Landing that new Club is an opportunity to improve weaknesses that may have been overlooked in the past, and can often be the very reason a new GM was brought in. Perhaps the board saw in you, as the new GM, the skills needed to not only detect weaknesses but also to fix them. But first, you have to find them. And once you do how will you prioritize them and get the buy-in needed to improve them from the team that is already in place, which can often be a problem?

Most Clubs have very loyal employees. And whereas they're in hospitality, they tend to be very nice, warm, caring people, at least on the surface. But what I tend to see sometimes is that like most companies, they're not very good coaches, at least in regards to expectations and training feedback; either positive or negative. And they sometimes lack the ability to pass some of the goals down to the rest of the folks and really motivate them by saying, "This might not be my personal view, but it's important that we take the Club here." And all of your departments have to be on the same page.

What I tend to see is where we might identify people with weaknesses in those first 90 days we spoke of previously, and it might not be their fault they are identified as so. Maybe the weak link has never been properly coached, or given the proper training or the tools needed to get to that next level. So they are stuck at a certain level and perhaps either resent it or it makes them melancholy in their work. And again, maybe it's just not their fault.

A lot of times what I tend to see is that management allows it to go on; they don't want to rock the boat or to upset anybody. But then, unfortunately, they are doing this employee a disservice because they're not being honest, but would rather live with the mindset of putting up with things until that person either leaves or retires. But in the interim what they are doing is putting pressure on the "chain."

The new GM is taking inventory of everything and everybody, determining who the rock stars are and who doesn't look like they are going to make the cut. But those that are the ones you have to focus on, to determine whether they deserve the chance to become a rock star, or at the very least more capable in their duties, or get cut from the team. Are they ready to jump onboard and be part of the mission statement and the long-term solution? Even if they haven't been coached, trained, or managed correctly.

Entitlement also comes into play. When I see employees who have been there 20 or more years, their mindset is, "What are you going to do with me? I know where the bodies are buried. I know the right people on the board." This means they also know who to complain to. These folks scare me as they are often the weak links. They do not want to change. They do not want to buy in. But we created the monster by allowing them to get away with murder all these years. And now you have somebody who's new telling them simple things like you have to get to work on time. You have to do your job. You have to do it safely. And, you have to do with a smile. That's when they dig their heels in and mumble under their breath, "Who are you to tell me this?" The question really is: How is that hurting the Club?

When people are stuck in this entitlement stage in their career, what I often see is that change is a four-letter word. The push back is don't innovate, don't change, even if it would make everything better, faster, cheaper, I don't really care. I'm in this mode. And they're just not willing to buy in, move forward, or collaborate. But sometimes pushback is good, as long as it's for a good cause. Is the pushback a result of just wanting to be a pain in the butt, or is it an offer to be challenged? I do like that and I always tell managers just because someone doesn't agree with you, it's not necessarily a bad thing. And if it moves things forward—if it strengthens the chain—why not?

Allow me to share a story. We recently worked with a non-tipping Club and the General Manager was hearing rumors of an employee who was getting tipped. Then the GM found out not only was he getting tipped by members, but he was also taking tips from other employees for services like helping them get the best schedule. It was a whole side business. But HR wouldn't let him go because he was loved by the membership. So, every other GM saw what was going on and let it go. Well, one incoming GM finally did get him fired, and he filed a wrongful termination and a workers' comp claim. I actually told them congratulations, you fired a thief; someone who was killing the organization's morale by instituting favoritism. The change of taking away that toxic individual was like a breath of fresh air for the Club. So why did this person survive for 25 years, even though everyone knew what he was doing? They all knew of him. But they were scared of him. He knew where the bodies were buried and exactly who he was going to complain to. But you need to remove the weaknesses. You need to remove the toxic people. You need to see who's pulling down everyone else or you're never going to progress or go in the right direction.

I have another story that hits home. We have a client who has an events director who brings in $2 million in revenue annually, and as far as the Club is concerned she could walk on water. But it also so happens that she is the nastiest person in the world. She's nice to those that can help her; she's strategic in that way. But she also has these tantrums. When she gets angry, she's yelling and screaming to the point where she's on the verge of employee harassment. It got so bad that we were seeing top department heads leaving because of her complaining and the hostile work environment she was creating. She was the weak link. We looked at the financials and we saw her bringing in $2 million. My answer to that was if she had a nice personality, she could probably bring in $4 million. I said this person is so toxic to everyone else, is she worth disrupting the team for? You have to look at the totality of what's happening and ask yourself, "Is it all worth it?"

Your job as the new GM is keeping things happy at home, that's really what the board wants to see. Members want to come and relax in their Club and not have to take a vote on the color of the napkins or pick out the carpet. Most people just want to come and relax and enjoy themselves and not feel like their home away from home is not being managed properly. And if people are talking to me and telling me something in my ear, or I'm getting these notices of this happening and that happening, they start to doubt things are being run well. And that's a direction you don't want to see your tenure heading in because it will quickly become a train wreck.

I would say that when a new GM comes in, the controller or CFO needs to provide a clear and concise overview of the numbers and explain the budget and the short falls- if any. Controlling and understanding the finances is critical and if miss managed- you'll find not only the Treasurer and Finance Committee breathing down your neck, you'll also see two more sub-committees being developed to help monitor the situation. Having a controller by your side to keep a watchful eye over the departments and finances is a critical piece when looking at collaboration and trust. The other one is HR. I believe that every GM should sit down with each and every employee, shake their hand, and understand what it is they do. And I think they need to ask; do you feel comfortable? Do you feel safe? Do you think you're being treated fair? Do you have an outlet? And what I have found is that just by talking to a few employees and trying to get some honest feedback you will really get a good pulse on the employees. They also should be able to comfortably say whatever they're thinking.

When speaking with the HR Director, you can ask, "Hey, correct me if I'm wrong, but I'm told these 12 folks are worth keeping an eye on. Are you seeing that as well?" If the answer is yes, then you can ask if they have been written up. If the HR person says, "Well, we haven't done that yet, although I believe that they are a weak link in the organization." Then pretty quickly you can see that they have an HR person who is protecting them and not protecting the Club. That's not a good thing.

As a new GM, the HR person is your direct link to finding the weak link. In a heartbeat that person should be able to spit out without hesitation; here's the rookies, here's who's disabled, here's your prima donna nobody wants to work with, here's the one always out on disability and won't be able to work for two months, here's two people that are set to retire, and so on. And if your HR person can't do that, why do you even have them? Anyone can put up posters and hand out employee manuals. What you need is someone who can assist you in identifying the best staff members working with teams and those who are the weaknesses. A really good HR person should be able to identify and strategize with you.

But don't see this as an attempt to "gather up the usual suspects" just to trim some fat. No new GM wants to go in and start firing people; a morale killer of the highest degree. Think of these challenging people as projects and let's see if we can turn them from the Dark Side. Because, if we don't turn them around, and decide instead to take an employment action, we're going to have the face the wrath of people who love these people, who likely don't know their HR background. If anything, what I like to tell people is I'm going to help you. Almost think of it as if I'm a teacher and I have someone who's failing in class. As we mentioned previously, the good students don't need that extra hour after class. But there are those that do.

Do I just give up and say you can't graduate? Or do I say see me after school? Let me give you a curriculum. Let's watch some videos. I'm going to give you this book. My job is to turn them around and bring them in closer to the overall mission. I always tell people; we're making them into little HR projects and giving them every opportunity to get better, to come onboard. I tell them what we want you to be happy. Life is too short. If you're miserable eight hours a day here; we're going to feel it. And we're not changing. Here's where we're going. You can join us.

The end game here is that HR needs to help department heads with their challenges before they become challenges. "Hey, how are those three new people you hired? Are they good? Are they bad? What's happening?" If a response from a department is that they are having some challenges, the knee-jerk reaction is to fire them. But that's not the plan of action to undertake. Maybe they're just employees in the wrong job?

I believe that to exist and thrive in the hospitality industry you need to have a service mindset, especially if you're interfacing with members. But you *have* to have that service heart; you can't fake it over time. And if you find that person who is *trying* to fake it; then you just found your weak link.

Action Points:

- Analyze your 90 day assessment

- Check in with your HR Department

- Identify your HR projects

A Final Thought:

"I won't accept anything less than the best a player's capable of doing and he has the right to expect the best that I can do for him and the team!" - Lou Holtz

CHAPTER 6

The Team Captain Calls the Plays

"When you're GOOD at something, you'll tell everyone.
When you're GREAT at something, they'll tell you."
- Walter Payton

The football coach rules the roost. He is the one giving the instructions on how things will be run, whether it's on the practice field, in a team meeting, or on the sidelines during a game. But his influence never crosses the sidelines during a game. He's not in the offensive huddle, or barking out orders on the defensive line while the opposition is setting up, or making sure players are lined up correctly on special teams. It's between the lines where the captains create their influence. And the same can be said for the Club hierarchy.

Within the infrastructure of a Club, this key person is not necessarily going to have the title of manager or supervisor, but that doesn't make him/her any less influential. This is usually a person who is trusted and respected by many, a person that knows the ins and outs of the Club. He/she knows who the important players are at the Club, and they might actually be the ones that train people how to do their job and decide who does what and when. And depending on who this person is, they can actually help management or hurt management.

For any new incoming GM, it's important to try to find out who these people are. They're usually somebody who's being sought out if there are any new rules, policies and/or procedures put in place. Employees will seek out their counsel; is this good, should we be worried, what's your take on this? This person is the point of the spear when it comes to gathering information on issues facing the Club.

Let's use workplace injuries as an example. Imagine we are starting to experience a wave of workers' compensation claims and we are trying to determine the causes of these injuries. We start by talking with the manager and supervisor, but we're really not getting any sort of positive feedback or anything substantial that we can put our arms around. We start asking the employee who is in charge of safety here, and who's a spokesperson for all of you that we can talk to, and then we can find out how to keep you safe.

We faced this same scenario at a particular Club and we actually had four or five employees tell us we should talk to Hector. We found out that Hector was not a manager and not a supervisor, but just a loyal employee that a lot of people respected because he had been at the Club just over 25 years. So now we knew who to talk to regarding what the problems were. We were getting absolutely nowhere with management; they couldn't identify anything. Probably within 10 minutes of talking to Hector we actually found out that various pieces of equipment were broken, although they had been reported to management numerous times. We found out that a couple of employees were unhappy because management didn't care about their safety. And as an added bonus, we also found out a few disgruntled people were stealing from the Club. He also added that the one thing we could do to show the employees we appreciated them was every now and then do a luncheon for the employees, that it would really help morale. In the end, we got more information out of Hector in 10 minutes then spending an entire morning with the managers.

Hector was able to identify and help us really correct some of the issues, but then he was also valuable as a voice of the people. When we began looking into instilling a vision, with a new mission and new goals, one of the things that we needed to do was to make sure that Hector was onboard, as well as the managers and supervisors. We needed everyone that had these critical influential relationships onboard, so that they could actually communicate it down to everyone else.

The next logical question is: Does this ever create a jealousy factor among the managers if the GM is going to somebody below them to get information? Possibly. But the GM's commitment is the wellbeing of the Club, and if the new GM wants to get a feel of the pulse and on the morale, then he needs to know who the key players are. And if you are a really good manager, then you need to put your ego aside and also befriend this person.

This Team Captain can keep people in line by saying, "Hey, you're making us all look bad." But at the same time if you treat a family member wrong—and you'll find that nepotism runs rampant in Clubs—then he can easily turn against you. But what I tend to see is that this person is really trying to create a good culture where everybody understands the credo, the motto; where everyone is moving in the same direction. And when you put together safety committee meetings, make it a point to ask them to help pick a good cross section of people, because it usually isn't your managers and supervisors getting hurt because they aren't the ones doing the actual job. This cross-section of employees is going to be your eyes and ears. And by giving them that little extra added responsibility they may say to themselves, "You know, I may not have that title, but I'm pretty important. And also people do listen to me." Because at the end of the day you want them to be safe and happy. You want them to understand and emulate the culture that you're trying to bring into the Club.

Sadly, as in most things in life, there are two sides to a coin. Here's an example: We had a Club client that had a Team Captain that was in the golf department. He was very charismatic, was loved by the members, was loved by the board, and could put on a real show. However, he was totally feared by employees and a veteran employee for almost 25 years. In fact, it was discussed that he complained about the Club, the GM, and the other managers and did everything possible to derail any growth or improvements at the Club. But because he was beloved by the members, the Club was reluctant to let him go because members would be upset. Now, it wouldn't be so bad if this person was part of the kitchen staff, because nobody would see him. But he was right out-front interacting with members and almost rubbing it in the face of management. He was what we would call a negative influencer, and they thought there's nothing they could ever do about him.

When it actually came to light how negative and toxic this person was, management was very cautious because of his contacts; "How can we actually take an employment action against him?" And I said if you don't, then you are going to let everyone else who has exposure to him know that this is okay; you are setting a precedent. You're saying to your employees, "We really don't care about you. We know he doesn't respect you, which means *we* don't respect you." In essence, what he is doing is holding the Club hostage to this toxic environment.

Finally, the Club had no choice but to let this individual go, and as predicted they got hit with workers' comp claims and legal dust-ups. What did they expect? He was a negative and toxic individual that was getting worse with age. I congratulated them for doing something that should have been done 25 years ago,

Team Captains are influencers. The question is, are they going to help you push forward and help the culture become healthy? Are they going to help you see your vision? Or do you have people in place that are going to try and obstruct everything you try to put in place; new policies, procedure, new goals, your mission statement, everything you need to do to take the Club to that next level? Are they going to influence people in a positive way or in a negative way?

I always refer to these people as very big HR projects because not only do you have to deal with them, but you have to deal with all these other people that they may have dominion over as well. But you will find with the negative influencers that if you extract that cancerous part of the organization, there are actually a lot happier and relieved people in the end.

But one of the first mistakes new GMs often make is to pretend these people don't exist. Or, if they do, that they are a mere minor annoyance and easily brushed aside, that their opinion is of no value. And if that be the case, I would say that, unfortunately, all the wonderful things you're doing at this level are going to start to break down as you move down the management chain. Picture it, you're envisioning this Shangri-La and then you're passing it down to your leadership team and they're onboard. But that team then has to infiltrate it down to the line people. And if you have a very powerful person dominating the line employees, it stops right there. Like hitting a brick wall. And you probably won't ever know it because as far as you know, the mid-level managers and the leadership team are doing their job of passing it down. But is it really being communicated? Is it really being felt by the employees or is it being deflected from what you're trying to do and perhaps also being sabotaged? Hopefully that influencer is somebody you've connected with and has said to you, "How can we get better?" I think ultimately these Team Captains want to be sounding boards, which they interpret as being respected. They want you to ask how can we get better? How can we help you? How can we be safer? In the end they don't want a big title; they just want to be part of the process.

I really do think that an employee advisory group is important to see what your core values are. Are people happy? Do they have a sense of belonging? You actually may find out that there are some real gems within that committee that could have a future in a managerial role.

Sometimes you have to go above and beyond. I meet up periodically with the risk manager at the Beverly Hills Hotel and she was beaming about all of their employee programs. She then directed me to the entrance for the employees. It was the employee "red carpet" entrance. It mirrored the iconic carpet at the front of the hotel where celebrities and wanna-be celebrities take their photos. Not only is it beautiful it highlights the true stars; the employees. They aligned the guest experience with the employee arrival to enhance morale, motivation and increase engagement. You look at the employee entrance of your average Club and it's in a back alley near the rear door of the kitchen. You can see the care and concern and the effort that's put into building employee morale on behalf of the hotel, and you can bet their influencers have taken notice. At the end of the day do you have internal influencers that continue to bring to light your vision and support the goals to the souls and hearts of the employees?

Action Points:

- Identify your internal leaders
- Ask your internal leaders for their feedback and suggestions
- Create an employee advisory group

A Final Thought:

"We have no difficulty finding the leaders: they have people following them." - William Gore

CHAPTER 7

Game Day Stress

"You FAIL all of the time. But you aren't a FAILURE until you start blaming someone else."- Bum Phillips

When you become a Club General Manager it's important to know your ABC's, or rather your ADA, CFRA, FMLA, HIPPA, FLSA, DFEH, EPSLA, and FFCRA's. Because next to the Tooth-Billed Pigeon and the Kakapo Parrot, the American Employee is perhaps the most protected species on the planet.

The government has never met an acronym it didn't like, and there are numerous ones now in play to safeguard the well-being of your workers, whether it's due to stress, mental illness, physical illness, financial illness, or just good old-fashioned "We're having a baby!" Throw in anxiety and depression, and you have created a virtual bouillabaisse of reasons you might someday get a phone call from an employee telling you they will be out of work for six months "due to personal reasons." And right in the middle of your busy season.

We live in a stressful world, and it's unrealistic to think your employees are going to park that stress at the time clock when they punch in for the day. They could be dealing with the three D's (Death, Divorce, Debt), or something much deeper and more complex. Sometimes it takes you down and sometimes it makes you more resilient. So, you have someone who's clocking in and out and coming to work eight hours a day, but are they really there? Are they really functioning? Can they focus? Do they have bill collectors calling them at all times of the day and night (including during work hours)? Are they constantly thinking about all the stresses of life and not able to do a quality job? Unfortunately, just because you clock in doesn't mean those stresses clock out.

In order to have a game-winning game-plan, you have to minimize the amount of people on the injured list (IL). But it's also important to gauge the way you react to that IL. If your reaction is something akin to, "Well, *I* have a bad back and *I'm* still working," then you better hope you didn't say it too loud, because other employees are taking stock in how you react. I know that as a supervisor you're worried about the schedule, but look at it from their side. What if somebody is having a nervous breakdown and you've been notified they have this ailment and they can't do 100% of their job. Do you want them at work? These are your players and it's part of your job to make sure they are in the right frame of mind physically and mentally to do their job.

So, what are the warning signs that an employee may be off his game? Is it somebody who is traditionally always on time but now punching in late? Is their productivity lacking? Are they frequently on their cell phone during the day? Has there been deterioration in the way they dress, personal hygiene, and an increased lack of organization? Do they seem like they just... don't... care? These may seem like little teeny signs, but they could also be the tip of an emotional iceberg. And if you don't see some of those signs or recognize some of those signs, and attempt to help resolve some of the symptoms, you may have somebody that clearly goes out for six months during your busy time.

For example, one of the busiest times for a golf club is their annual member/guest event. Everyone comes out and you're showcasing your property. The members are showing off to their friends and family all of the perks of being a member. Now what if you had one of your team members, someone that knows your department through and through, who is one of your star players, and he says, "I have to leave. I can't come back for six weeks." Would you freak out without even knowing their back story? I get it; you're worried about the schedule. It's the busiest time of the year and you need all hands-on deck. In fact, you've got two people that are already out, so you're maxed out. Take a breath.

How you react to this person that is asking for a medical leave and it's almost irrelevant whether it's true or their story has more holes than a Life Savers factory, is everything. I always remind Club managers and supervisors that if someone comes to you and says, "Hey, I have to be on medical leave," *do not go with your gut feeling.* That's when you have to put on your HR hat and ask yourself what would HR say in a situation like this? HR would say, okay, can you tell me a little bit more? Can you tell me the extent of how much time do you need? At the end of the day, I tell managers and supervisors to pass the hot potato to HR. You really don't want to get into the nitty-gritty of hearing that somebody's grandfather has prostate cancer. Your response should be, "I'm so sorry to hear that. We're a little crazy right now and I'm not familiar with all the leaves. I don't have the employee manual memorized. I don't know if we can or can't, so why don't we take this to HR, alright?" Human nature is that you will have an initial reaction, but don't say it. It's like writing that angry email; just walk away before you hit send. You can't unring that bell. Best rule is to grit your teeth, send the employee to HR, and then, if it makes you feel better, go into the restroom and scream.

Once the employee gets to HR, the first question will be if they need a doctor's note. Now here the HIPPA Gods will protect the reason for the leave, but a doctor's note will at least establish, officially, that this employee is unable to perform his job duties, whether for physical, mental or emotional reasons. There are many different protected leaves; pregnancy, alcoholism, the list goes on. But no matter what the reason, they are called protected leaves for a reason; you have to protect their job. There is a saying in sports that no player should lose his position because he's injured, meaning when he returns, no matter how good his replacement performs, that injured player must have a shot at keeping his old job. Of course there are exceptions to the rule. In 2001 in the fourth quarter of the Jets-Patriots game, Jets linebacker Mo Lewis slammed into Patriots quarterback Drew Bledsoe along the right sideline and put him out of action. In steps backup quarterback Tom Brady and Bledsoe never got his job back as Brady led the Patriots to their first of six Super Bowl titles. But the story has a quasi-happy ending; Bledsoe was traded to the Buffalo Bills in the off-season and made the Pro Bowl in 2002.

But this is the exception, not the rule. The bottom-line is this: You have to protect their job. Tread carefully and make sure you're monitoring how people are reacting. I think the intake and the response is critical because you have to remember that people talk. Twenty years ago, they talked in the lunchroom. Today they talk on social media.

Let's say we have a beloved locker room attendant named Rosie. Not a great employee; but we give her numerous chances because she's beloved and knows all the right members. Then we have somebody else who doesn't interface with that many members. And we don't give that person as much time. I always tell people what you do for one, you do for all. And when someone comes to you for medical purposes, you treat the situation the same; don't cherry pick which ones you are okay with and which ones you aren't.

I really do believe that the documentation and the interactive process needs to be clear, concise, and documented. The one thing that I usually see while people are on leave is that managers come back with a full list of issues, such as they've never been a good employee, or this temp is running circles around them, or I found all these mistakes. But no matter what emerges during the leave, you can't fire them. There are no Tom Brady's on your team. It's called protected leave for a reason. People have asked me, should I fire her before she leaves the hospital or when she comes back? And I always say, "Do you see something wrong with this timing?" Okay, so she's not perfect and she's been written up a few times. Once she comes back to work, and if the behavior for the first and second grievance or issue continues, then you are on solid footing. But don't dump a wheelbarrow full of complaints on that person's lap the first day back on the job. It just doesn't look right on the surface of it. You want to avoid a discrimination and/or harassment type of claim when someone's on a leave.

Also worth noting, do not try and self-diagnose the medical reason someone needs to go out on leave. You need something from a medical professional, a required certification of doctor's notes, to approve some sort of leave. Then you can plan accordingly should the leave extend indefinitely. On the other hand, I always tell my clients just because you get a doctor's note doesn't mean you can have leave forever. There usually has to be some kind of end point, but I do tell people all the time you need to get something from the doctor now, especially if you think it's totally bogus. However, be prepared for some possible pushback: "What, you don't trust me?" Trust isn't the issue. You need medical certification so that you have an idea, based on their job description and their ability to lift, push, pull, if this is going to be episodic? Will it be for a long period? So that way you are not handcuffed in regards to not being able to do your job and manage the workforce, to map out a plan.

Don't be surprised if the employee throws HIPPA laws in your face; "Why do I have to tell you what's wrong with me?" The easy comeback is "I don't want to know the name of whatever you have. I just want to know your limitations."

In California alone, there are at least 20 or more protected leaves, everything from donating bone marrow to being a volunteer firefighter. But documentation is key. If that employee is on a leave because their mother is sick; it doesn't affect them doing their physical job when they return. If they are out on leave because the cartilage in their knee has turned to oatmeal, that sets up a different dynamic. But again, it's one of those things where you need to be consistent. You can't cherry pick and say they look like a liar because while doing social media searches you saw them walking around the mall. If you do that then I am going to ask, "Okay, well, was he lifting, pushing, pulling anything? No? Well, that's what his restrictions are. Maybe walking is part of his rehab." Of course, if Mr. Oatmeal Knee is on Instagram climbing the North Face, perhaps there's room for doubt. But try not to go there. For family medical leave (FMLA), you can actually attach a job description to the medical certification because a doctor really is blind to what the job is the patient is doing.

One of the key things is to do what you can to avoid such a situation by creating a paternal responsibility within all departments and being both empathetic and compassionate, especially if you are seeing productivity lag, more absenteeism, and deterioration in the quality of work. Or maybe they are just not as engaged. Ask if everything is okay. Remind them that you offer all these benefits, such as an employee assistance program, onsite counseling, stress management classes, etc. Don't let it get to the point that what you have to offer won't suffice. It will also be much easier to make that connection if they do feel comfortable coming to you. Then, you can say, "I'm not familiar with all the different leaves. Why don't we go to HR? They might ask you more questions and may be able to provide you with more information."

I can't stress enough not to freak out and start screaming, "Oh my God, this is my senior person. What am I going to do?" You may feel like you are on the way to the Super Bowl and now your star quarterback is sidelined with a shoulder injury. But while you're running around bemoaning about the sky falling, you are being watched by other employees who may someday be in that very same position. If people see managers ragging inappropriately, and caring more about their situation than that of the employee, it gives off the air that the company doesn't care. And if that person watching is somebody who is also dealing with hardship, anxiety, stress, and depression, or an illness of a family member, they're going to become more stressed.

Interestingly, a lot of Clubs have resources available for members. After all they pay the freight and keep the lights on. You want to keep them well. But it's important to understand that healthy and happy employees will give a better member experience. These are the Clubs that get it, that reinvest in their employees. You see them doing campaigns for flu shots. You see them doing campaigns for a breast cancer awareness month or health fairs, and stretching before work, and how to have healthy lunch and everything that goes with it. It's all about creating a caring environment. And trust me; members notice how Clubs treat their staff. It may not be obvious; but it is there.

In conclusion; I work with a company and one day as I was walking around their offices I saw several empty rooms. When I inquired what they were for I was told it was for the psychologists and psychiatrists that come in once a month to meet with the management team. When I asked them why they felt that was important they replied, "These are the most important people in our organization. We can't have them out. We need to give them the support they need."

Is that how you feel about your employees?

Action Points:

- Train your managers on HR Basics
- Know and understand protected leaves
- Create an employee wellness campaign

A Final Thought:

"A good objective of leadership is to help those who are doing poorly to do well and to help those who are doing well to do even better." - Jim Rohn

CHAPTER 8

Defending an Oncoming Blitz

"It takes 20 YEARS to build a reputation, and 5 MINUTES to ruin it."- Peyton Manning

In the opening monologue from the film, *The Blind Side*, we are told that the highest paid player on an NFL team is the quarterback. But what most people probably don't know is the second highest paid player is usually the left tackle. This is because the left tackle's job is to protect the quarterback from what he can't see coming. And what that quarterback can't see coming is pretty much the same thing a Club GM can't see either, and that is a potentially devastating hit that could end a career. For the QB, the blow comes courtesy of a freight train disguised as a 300-lb linebacker. For the Club GM, the hit that could potentially put your Club at high risk comes in the form of a key event that goes astray, bad employee behavior (and bad member behavior), bad press, EPA and OSHA violations, or just anything that earns the ire of the surrounding community. In essence, any risk that could take the Club down and/or result in litigation.

It's a simple question; what keeps you up at night? Because even if you can think of five things that keep you awake, be assured there are another half-dozen things you *don't* know about lurking on the edges. Because, as someone once pointed out, you don't know what you don't know. Don't get into the misguided mindset of, "If I've never experienced it, it's not really a big problem." Maybe you've been at a big Club for 20 years and you've been though all the wars; fires, OSHA, discrimination cases, and so forth. And it's fine that you've had the opportunity to learn and grow through these experiences. But it is also safe to say there are still areas of risk that can pop up at anytime, when you least expect it, in places you never thought it would ever happen.

When they do emerge, and they will, do you have a good offensive line in place to protect your quarterback? Whether you do or you don't, you still need to know where your risk is and put together a plan with full knowledge that different Clubs have different risks based on size, demographics, location, etc. Maybe your team isn't at full-strength to deal with the next risk coming in from the blind side because one of your key offensive linemen is hobbled by an ugly million-dollar lawsuit, or you have four or five players out on workers' compensation leave and your insurance premiums have doubled. Whatever situation you are currently dealing with, it's imperative that when that Next Big Risk hits, even if your team isn't at full-strength, that there has to be a really clear focus on what needs to be addressed at your Club. For example, if a new GM is coming in and nobody knows what they're supposed to be doing, or people are not being written up because of bad performance, or you have managers that don't like to manage or lead, well, then you're going to see a really bad reaction when risk occurs. And the likely fallout from this swing-and-miss response is you are going to also see a really bad member experience.

Most of the times when I sit down and talk with Clubs in regards to what do you want to work on; the usual response is the employee manual. Unfortunately, it's usually a pressing time-sensitive urgent item because something bad just happened. So now they're being more reactive than proactive.

When it comes to Private Clubs, as it does in most businesses, crisis management is a hot topic. It was a hot topic pre-COVID, and now it burns like red-hot coals. Along with figuring out what to do in the midst of a once in a generation pandemic, you still have to worry about what to do with no electricity, or what do if you do if you have an employee that is having a heart attack, or if there's on the job violence. It's all about how are you reacting? How quickly and effective is your communication process so the authorities aren't flooded by the same 911 call? Do you have proper overall safety protocols in place to avoid any sort of injury mishaps (i.e. proper first-aid training)? Sadly, we live in a litigious society, where people want to sue restaurants because they spilled hot coffee on themselves getting into their car.

Some of the more inherent risks don't come in the shape of OSHA visits, earthquakes and members having a stroke on the 14th green, but instead they can be initiated by how your employees are treated or are perceived to have been treated, especially in the hiring and firing stage. Have you accumulated proper documentation if you need to fire an employee, something that can serve as a protective moat when lawyers start storming the Club? Also one key is dealing with employees as it relates to leaves, whether it is for medical reasons or mental health reasons (see previous chapter). The biggest area that general managers can really focus in on is giving their managers and supervisors the tools to respond appropriately, professionally and with empathy as cases arise. And this comes back to understanding the hiring process.

Let's start with the job description (the first step in avoiding a potential employee-centric risk). So how do you actually create a job description? You do this by clearly spelling out that these are essential job functions; no if ands or buts, these tasks are requirements to do this particular job. You don't want to hire someone unless they can do the job. And I don't think that you should keep them around unless they can do the job. But should that occur, that a dismissal is warranted, be prepared for blowback; "It must be because of my age, race, creed, color, national origin." And your response should be, "No, this is the job. You knew what the job involved before you were hired, and what was required. You did not do your job. Therefore…"

I think for the most part most general managers and department heads do a good job avoiding risk by telling the new hires that they're going to be trained for two weeks, and after the third week we'll sit down and discuss if there are any problems we should address. This way nothing festers. You now have a process in place to find out whether or not they are going to be a good team member and whether or not you hired the right person. Your hiring process is critical for success and it must be crafted carefully and followed to the letter to ensure that success.

Remember, timing is everything because any of your employment decisions could on the surface look like retaliation, even though the employee you are eye-balling continually goes out on leave or frequently or ends up with a workers' comp case at the drop of a hat. Or maybe there are some issues between employees that might start out as joking and kidding around but eventually erupts into on the job violence. Here's a perfect example, I once worked with a Club where there was a lot of joking around in the kitchen, with horseplay and name calling, which is frequent in this industry. But things were getting heated and the managers and supervisors didn't put a stop to it; nip it in the bud, so to speak. And it kept escalating. The employee complained to the Head Chef that he was being harassed, but no action was taken. Instead the response was, "Well, do you want to work the hours or not?" The worker said he did and went back to work in the kitchen. A few hours later that emotional dam burst; the employee attacked his tormenter, killing him in front of not only the other employees but also members. What seemed like innocent banter turned into a tragic event.

More than anything you think to yourself; could this have been avoided? Perhaps what was considered light ribbing years ago isn't as acceptable in the times we now live in. And at the end of the day it is no longer how you say something, but what you actually say. It's not a stretch to suggest that people are more sensitive now to what they hear than they might have been in the past. And it's your job to know where that threshold is because everything you do is being recorded someplace by a camera. And what you think may be something said in jest could actually be considered harassment.

As much as you need to be conscious of internal risks, there is also a wary eye that needs to be placed on outside forces. You are dealing with outside vendors on a constant basis, which lends itself to a whole list of potential problems. But there's also exposure to membership and guests as well. It's your job to create a wonderful member experience, but at the same time you have to be conscious of potential risk. So, while your employees are doing a good job working safely around garden equipment and chemicals, which goes back to proper training, they also have to be alert to member-centric risk. Timeliness is everything. What if a member is out on the green and suddenly suffering from heat stroke and they refuse to go to the hospital? What if he passes out while he's out there? Or worse, passes away?

This is where crisis management comes into play? Does the employee know what to do? Does he or she know how to fill out an incident report? Or at the very least, who to call? There needs to be an emergency plan in place that becomes second nature to any employee who becomes unfortunately involved with such a potential risk. Because, no response, and even the wrong response, could have dire consequences for the Club.

As a Club's General Manager, you have to anticipate what's going to happen before it happens, even though soothsayer may not have been in your job description when you were hired. It's like when you live and work in California, you know eventually you're going to have The Big One. So, when the ground starts shifting, do you know where your emergency kits are? Do you know where to turn off the gas? You know you're going to have slips and falls, maybe in the kitchen or a locker room, and you know you're going to have members take ill, because everyone knows that a golf course is a very popular place to have heart attacks. And they never happen in the clubhouse. I would say train your staff in emergency crisis management and use your cell phone as tools, especially if there were to be somebody who comes onto the premises with a gun. What is the protocol? You don't want 25 people calling 911. You need one person who's in charge.

I would say to anticipate the top areas of crisis management starting with things that you've experienced; are you doing the fire drills and earthquake drills? Are you practicing how to use the fire extinguisher? Everything should be a habit, so that your people feel comfortable.

Truth be told, you can't *avoid* all risk, but you should be *anticipating* all risks. If your Club was located in Tornado Alley you'd know who gets all of the equipment indoors and how fast and how to secure it? That should be a no brainer. And who's going to take the lead? This may be the most important question that needs to be answered, because timeliness is the key when it comes to making decisions.

Here's another example of a risk a general manager might not see coming. I had a client who had a member loading himself up with an oil-based sunscreen in the restroom, which was used by both members and employees. This guy turned the floor of the men's room into an ice-skating rink. People were coming in and just literally falling and hitting their heads. How do you foresee something like that? It was just one of those things where the person didn't do it outside where people normally do it. I'm sure if you looked in the employee manual about what to do if someone sprays sunscreen all over the restroom floor; you're not going to find that notation. However, was this the first time or did it happen in the past? Break the pattern especially if you've experienced it and felt the impact.

It's imperative that you look around your Club, identify the hazards, and then do what it takes to either prevent them or train your employees on how to react should they occur. Think of it like baby proofing your house before your two-year old grandchild visits. It's just easier to stop something from happening in the first place than to repair the damage after it has happened.

Action Points:

- Look at previous risk and exposures along with the impact

- Identify your new risk and exposures

- Plan, prepare and train your leaders and staff

A Final Thought:

"Risk is like fire: If controlled it will help you; if uncontrolled it will rise up and destroy you." - Theodore Roosevelt

CHAPTER 9

Avoiding a Penalty Flag

"It's not whether you get knocked DOWN,
it's whether you get UP. "- Vince Lombardi

To say we live in an ever-evolving litigious society, where peoples' first inclination is to reap the rewards for what they perceive to be an injustice is a gross understatement. All you have to do is turn on daytime TV to be inundated with a virtual tsunami of ads by attorneys offering the viewer monetary retribution (*"Although we accept no payment until settlement"*), all in the name of righting that perceived wrong.

If you're the GM of a Club, a lawsuit brought forth can cost you time, money, productivity, undue stress and a serious dent in employee (and quite possibly member) morale. Think of an employee lawsuit as a rock dropped in a stream, with the rippling effect spreading out over all your departments, from food & beverage to landscaping and maintenance. Back in the day when an employee sued their Club it could be kept under wraps. Mark Zuckerberg pretty much killed that idea back in 2004.

Employee lawsuits can also be learning experiences from which to gain wisdom, admittedly at a cost. But before we determine the steps needed to avoid them, we need to first address some of the reasons they are brought forth.

According to *Employment Benefit Adviser*, these are the top 10 business practices that can get an employer sued:

1. Incorrectly identifying the employer

Employee handbooks often incorrectly identify the employer. Handbooks are often drafted without proper attention to maintaining strict separation between corporations and this may complicate efforts to defend against employment claims. Audit agreements and payroll practices to review whether corporate separation is being maintained include employee handbooks, pay checks, W-2 forms, non-competition agreements, nondisclosure agreements and invention agreements.

2. Failing to make individualized determinations on criminal convictions

Arrests versus criminal convictions on an employee's resume or work history can be two separate subjects. Criminal convictions are reliable evidence of criminal conduct, while arrests alone are not evidence of a crime. A criminal conviction requires proof beyond a reasonable doubt and arrests cannot be used to exclude an individual from employment except under very rare circumstances, according to the EEOC.

Many states take the position that an employer cannot automatically exclude an employee or applicant with a criminal conviction.

3. Faulty timekeeping practices

An employer must keep records of all work time the employer knows about or has reason to know about regardless of the time an employee is required or asked to work. Keeping accurate track of all the time a nonexempt employee works each workday and each workweek will deter unpaid work discrepancies.

If off-the-clock work occurs, the employee must be paid for all hours worked. Time records should be corrected to reflect actual hours worked and then employers may enforce policies with disciplinary measures, if appropriate. Avoid automatic deductions, and editing time punches should only be done by an authorized manager and always double-check with the employee.

4. Improper deductions from pay

The salary basis rule requires that exempt employees must receive a predetermined amount of pay for every work week in which they perform any work. Deductions may not be made for absences occasioned by the employer or by the operating requirements of the business. Improper deductions include deduction for a partial-day absence to attend a family matter, deduction of a day of pay because the employer was closed due to inclement weather, deduction of three days of pay because the employee was absent from work for jury duty and deduction for a two-day absence due to a minor illness when the employer does not provide wage replacement benefits for such absences.

5. Overusing independent contractors

There is no bright line rule regarding who is an independent contractor. There are different tests depending on the forum the employer is in to determine if they are using an independent contractor. These tests include the IRS 20-point test, the Economic Realities test and the Right of Control test.

In the event of a case between an employer and an independent contractor, the DOL and courts will consider whether the individual's work is an integral part of an employer's business, the amount of the individual's investment in facilities and equipment, whether the individual has any real opportunities for profit and loss, whether the individual exercises initiative, judgment, foresight, skills and initiative in the business sense, whether the relationship is permanent or indefinite.

6. Marijuana laws and employment practices

As of November 2020, 36 states and the District of Columbia have legalized marijuana to varying degrees and 53% of Americans support marijuana legalization, according to the Pew Research Center. Marijuana remains a Schedule I substance under the Federal Controlled Substance Act, which criminalizes the possession, manufacture, distribution and sale of the drug. However, many states have created marijuana-related employment protections such as private causes of action that prohibit employment discrimination or require reasonable accommodation of marijuana users under the Americans with Disabilities Act, and many medical marijuana users can claim to be disabled within the meaning of the ADA.

In states that prohibit employment discrimination or impose a duty to accommodate an employee's use, employers must analyze the specific needs of the job and competing federal laws and regulations. It is no longer safe to assume that marijuana's illegal status under federal law will prevent an employer from being sued or held under state law.

7. Light-duty accommodation for pregnancy

The Pregnancy Discrimination Act, or PDA, prohibits pregnancy-based discrimination and requires that pregnant employees be treated the same as other employees who are not so affected, but similar in their ability or inability to work. Pregnancy is not a disability, but the ADA Amendments Act of 2008 broadens the definition of disability, which potentially covers conditions related to pregnancy. These conditions can include pre-labor, hypertension, severe nausea, sciatica, gestational diabetes and certain complications from childbirth or miscarriage.

8. The Genetic Information Non-discrimination Act

Title II of the Genetic Information Non-discrimination Act prohibits employers from discriminating against employees, applicants and former employees based on genetic information. Employers can not deliberately acquire genetic information or disclose genetic information. Private sector employers with at least 15 employees as well as employment agencies, labor organizations, state and local governments, and the Congress and Executive branches of the Federal Government are covered by this law. GINA forbids discrimination on the basis of genetic information in any aspect of employment including hiring, firing, pay, job assignment, promotions, layoffs, training, fringe benefits and any other condition of employment.

9. Overlooking recent ADA accommodation trends

From 2006 to 2016, ADA charges increased by nearly 75%. Areas of the ADA as enforced by the EEOC that have led employers into lawsuits include inflexible leave policies, transfer and reassignment, working from home and drug testing or medical exams. Most recent EEOC settlements have ranged from $100,000 in March 2017 due to failure to allow an employee to return to work on a part-time basis as an accommodation or additional leave, to $20 million, the largest settlement to date, in July 2011 for an inflexible attendance policy.

10. Not reviewing pay practices to eliminate unexplained disparities in pay

Employers shall not discriminate between employees on the basis of sex for equal work, on jobs that require equal skill, effort and responsibility, except where such payment is made pursuant to seniority, merit system, measures earnings by quantity or quality of production; or differential based on any factor other than sex, according to the Equal Pay Act. There is no clear cause of the gender pay gap, but industry experts have pointed to contributing factors such as women leaving certain industries due to inflexible work schedules or alleged discrimination, women taking unpaid breaks in their career to care for children and women being less likely to negotiate pay, raises and promotions.

Employers should be utilizing equal pay audits, before employees start asking and before the new EEO-Report form is due; looking at discrepancies between comparable jobs; looking beyond hourly rate and salary, including bonuses and benefits, do not over-rely on the market rate; reviewing hiring practices; reviewing the performance evaluation processes; maintaining a consistent compensation system; and involving outside counsel for attorney-client privilege protection.

These are all valid reasons, but all also easily avoided by being conscientious about both your individual state laws and a little common sense and decency. Because, as an employer, you will have a bulls-eye on your back. How big that target is will be determined by how you conduct your business and your relationships with your employees. Whether that bulls-eye will be the size of a barn door or the size of a golf ball is for you to determine.

Truth be told, workers who have their sights set on getting something for nothing have always been part of our history, probably starting 400,000 years ago when some caveman out on a hunt claimed to "hurt his back" tossing a spear at a Woolly Mammoth, when all he really wanted was to go back to his cave and spend all day looking at paintings on his wall. Every company has that person, somewhere, waiting, checking out expensive vacation plans on Expedia. But that's a small sample size. The key is how to avoid dealing with a legal situation from the other 99.9% of employees pulling in a paycheck from your Club, especially when issues like discrimination, wage and hour violations, dangerous work conditions, and workers' compensation claims rear their ugly heads. This is why proper enforcement of Club policy and procedures plus diligent documentation is so critical.

You can have the best policies and training in the world, but you better make sure your managers and supervisors follow these Club policies. Make sure your HR and legal teams (see Chapter Eleven) are providing the proper protection and training for management. But most importantly, always remember you aren't dealing with employee # 686229; you are dealing with people, and like most people they want to know they are appreciated for the efforts they put forth. Which means you can shrink that bulls-eye to a pinpoint by implementing policies that lean more towards the carrot and less towards the stick.

It might be a good idea at some point to implement a behavioral reward system, one that both rewards excellent work and gives an employee a sense of both appreciation and gratification. It can be something as extravagant as box-seats to a baseball game, or as simple as saying "great job." When employees take pride in their work, a pride often fueled by recognition by those up the ladder, they tend to see the Club they work for as a close-knit family. And although there are certainly cases out there of disgruntled (and dysfunctional) family members tossing lawsuits at each other like legal hand grenades, I am betting the closer the family is the less likely there will be litigation.

Of course, there are ways to try and prevent a lawsuit from happening, even before an employee is hired. Hiring is the single most important step to creating a dynamic team. Most managers fail to look at the importance of this step and hire to fill a spot. We use the old saying all of the time.... Hire Slow and Fire Fast (with documentation of course). When looking at candidates are you really looking at their history, education, experience, timelines, titles and responsibilities? Even if someone is just a specimen on paper *you need to do your due diligence*. In fact, you need to prepare a detailed job description, do phone interviews, reference checks, and do behavioral open-ended interviews to really find out if you have a prime candidate. Even after all that, it's now time for some assessments. Why? Again, do you want the best candidate or the best *available* candidate? Are you doing behavior and personality assessments? I can't tell you how many people get a report back on a candidate and decide to go against the findings of the report because they just want a body; someone with a heartbeat. Then in a few months they find out those assessments were 100% correct and now they are stuck with either a workers' comp claim or a legal claim just waiting to happen.

After you're satisfied that you have a qualified candidate who can be part of the team, it's time for the conditional job offer. The key word is *conditional*. It's important that they know you're hiring them but the next steps are a background check, credit check, drug/alcohol and /or screening/ physical. You don't need to apply these to all candidates, but they should be done uniformly based on the job categories. For example: If you lift, push and pull 50 lbs 90% of the day, you need to make sure they can actually do the job. If you're handing large sums of money and have access to all of the petty cash and accounts, it may be wise to do a credit check. I'm a firm proponent of alcohol/drug screenings. I'm always surprised to see how many people test positive, bring in "not human" urine samples and can't make the 48-72 hour window to do a test. While your managers will want to fast track this candidate they love, don't compromise. If you have a drug/alcohol policy at your Club, please adhere and be consistent because you are probably going to want people who are not intoxicated while frying, cutting, or using hazardous chemicals at the Club.

Background checks are key components to track down information on prospective employees who might have a track record of leaving lawsuits in their wake. You can call previous employers and find out why they left (or were asked to leave). A credit check may help determine if the candidate is heavily in debt to the point where he may be looking for a "way out."

You may think your Club is like Teflon, where any lawsuit, no matter how seemingly frivolous, will fail to stick. But remember, even legal action that *doesn't* stick can cost anywhere from $50-$200,000 in just legal fees, valuable time away from the job, and negative publicity for your Club.

Action Points:

- Stay on top of Federal, State. County, Local and Industry regulations and laws

- Do a compliance check of your internal practices

- Create and maintain a successful hiring process followed by all departments

A Final Thought:

"It's hard to beat a team that never gives up." - Babe Ruth

CHAPTER 10
On the Injury List

"Today I will do what others WON'T, so tomorrow I can accomplish what others CAN'T"- Jerry Rice

As the parent of three young children, I'm always thinking about what is best for them. General Managers should use the same thought process when working with injured employees.

I'm not advocating treating employees like children; but you should look out for their best interests when managing them. Injured employees are unlikely to fully understand the complex workers' comp system. They don't know what consequences their choices will have. Like children running around the house with scissors.

The process of managing an injury claim begins long before an employee injury occurs. When there is a task around the house that needs doing, first I have to figure out who is capable of doing the job without potentially being injured. My 10-year old is strong enough to hold onto the leash if our 50-lb dog tries to run off, my six-year old is not. So, I don't "hire" my six-year old to walk the dog, knowing full well what the consequences might be.

The same thing needs to happen in your hiring practices. Unfortunately, when you decide to hire someone you often don't know their past medical history and physical condition. When you make the choice to hire someone, you should have a conditional offer of employment. This form lets them know that they have the job, but only so long as a doctor says they are physically able to perform substantially all of the essential functions of the job. Once they have completed the form, off they go to the doctor who will examine them and determine if they have any restrictions as to what they are being hired to do.

If they don't have any restrictions, they are good to start the job. If the doctor places restrictions on them, it is then up to *you* to determine if your Club can reasonably accommodate those restrictions. Once you know you have an employee who can perform their job safely, you are good to go. If you train them on how to do their job safely, they are unlikely to get injured. Do you have a training library to show and illustrate how to do the job the right way? Creating a library on some of your physically demanding jobs is a way to start off the orientation process and training on the right foot. Why not show how to properly rake the bunkers, move heavy golf bags off shelves, using a hole-cutter, and cleaning and moving heavy pots in the kitchen?

In most states you can direct employees to an occupational doctor of your choosing. It's important that you speak with your insurance agent about the rules in your state. Choosing the doctor may be the single most important thing you can do to effectively manage the costs of employee injuries. If you choose the wrong occupational doctor, all of the best practices you have set up for later in the process can become useless.

Once you find an occupational doctor, visit with them. Then have them visit with you. Let them see the lay of the land, what duties are being performed on a daily basis, and who is capable of doing them. Are they comfortable sending employees back to work with restrictions or are they inclined to send folks home for several days? Will they agree to see your employees quickly after they arrive at the clinic? Will they give you a comprehensive list of restrictions when an employee is injured so you can find suitable transitional work until they are ready to go back to full duty?

It's important that both you and the doctor understand that there are only three reasons an employee can't be at work doing *something:*

1) Hospitalization

2) On medication that makes it unsafe for them to get to and/or be at work

3) They are contagious

Otherwise, both you and the doctor should be committed to returning any injured employees back to work immediately.

Why is it important that they get back to work immediately? First, when an employee is at home rather than at work, the clock is ticking for them to start receiving lost wage benefits from the insurance company. There are 36 states that when you keep the claim "medical only," meaning that there are no lost wages paid by the insurance company, you receive a 70% discount for that employee injury on your experience mod.

Also, studies show that the longer an employee is out, the less likely it is that they will ever return to their job. By the time an employee is out 12 weeks, there is only a 50% chance they will *ever* return to work. When employees are home on a workers' comp claim, it's likely that they are lying around the house watching TV. Have you watched any daytime TV lately? Every commercial break has at least one ad for an attorney that *cares* about them and will get them what they are owed (operators are standing by).

If the doctor is committed to getting your employees returned for transitional duty, then you have to commit to finding work for them to do. It is common for employers to feel like they don't have any light duty work. Start by brainstorming the work that isn't getting done. Some employees would be great candidates to do some building projects, maintenance work, touch ups, sanitizing, and minor housekeeping. There is likely clerical work that they could help with, as well. Talk with your employees about how they could modify their jobs if they had a physical restriction.

If an employee has to be out of work, make sure that you are consistent in communicating with them. Almost every time an employee retains an attorney to help with a workers' compensation claim it is because they felt uncertain, scared or ignored. You can prevent all of these emotions by being very transparent about what is going to happen. Most employees who get injured on the job have never been hurt at work before. They don't know if there are co-pays or deductibles. They don't understand that the insurance company will pay all of their medical bills and even pay for their lost wages if they have to be out of work.

While an employee is in a transitional duty position, be sure to get updates from the doctor. Many light duty positions are less strenuous than the work the employee was doing prior to injury. You want to make sure they get back to full duty as soon as possible because you don't want them to get comfortable in their "new" job and wind up malingering on the claim.

One last critical step in this process is getting the Club managers and supervisors onboard. Many times an employee sees their supervisor as their boss, even if that supervisor has no direct hiring and firing authority. If a supervisor has a bad attitude toward an employee that is working with restrictions, it can sink your effort. When that employee is made to feel bad about the fact that they can't do 100% of the job, they are very likely to crawl into the arms of that attorney that cares for them.

Just like a parent with a child, dealing with injured employees requires compassion, but also firmness. The best path through an employee injury is that you communicate your expectations to that injured employee. If you have all the pieces in place, you will find that your injured employees will follow your lead and get back to work happy, healthy and productive more quickly and less expensively than you thought possible.

Like death and taxes, it is inevitable that when you have multiple employees out on workers' comp leave your premiums most likely will go up. But there are steps to help control those rising costs:

1. Early Reporting: Report any workplace-related accident or injury as soon as possible. Also put into place measures to avoid any similar occurrences.

2. Have a Pre-Arranged Medical Care Facility: Having a pre-arranged medical facility available (one that understands your business) can help your organization get your injured worker the care they need right away and possibly back to work faster. It also avoids any lengthy ER visits.

3. Implement a Safety and Health Program: Make sure to commit to safety training and enforcement in order to effectively reduce workplace accidents and injuries can be reduced. By doing so you will increase productivity, reduce claim costs and ultimately reduce your experience modification factor.

4. Endorse Pre-lnjury Employee Education: Teach your employees how to prevent or respond to a work-related injury. This will also improve their job satisfaction and hopefully any employee litigation. Education should be offered during new employee orientation and annually thereafter.

5. Keep in Contact with Injured Workers: We all want to feel like we are a valuable cog in the Club's machine, and employers who ensure that injured workers receive appropriate treatment and maintain compassionate contact during the recovery period will find that employees will return to work faster. Something as simple as a phone call can work wonders and reduce the chance of legal involvement in claims.

Injuries can happen almost anywhere, and the Club environment is no exception. Perhaps one of the more prevalent injuries is in slip and fall scenarios. It could be something spilled in the restaurant kitchen, water on a locker room floor, an unsecured rug on a freshly-waxed floor, or something as innocuous as the morning dew on a freshly-manicured green.

According to the U.S. Department of Labor, slips, trips and falls account for more than 95 million lost work days per year – about 65% of all work days lost. Could your Club take that kind of personnel hit, and survive?

There are a variety of situations that may cause slips, trips and falls, according to the DOL:

- Wet or greasy floors
- Dry floors with wood dust or powder

- Uneven walking surfaces
- Polished or freshly waxed floors
- Loose flooring, carpeting or mats
- Shoes with wet, muddy, greasy or oily soles
- Clutter
- Electrical cords or cables
- Damaged ladder steps
- Ramps and gang planks without skid-resistant surfaces
- Metal surfaces

Each bullet can initiate escalating insurance rates, an experience mod trending in the wrong direction, and a big target on your Club's back when OSHA pays a visit.

So, what to do? Here are some suggestions:

1) Create a clean workplace environment
This should be an ongoing procedure that is simply done as part of each worker's daily performance. Know what needs to be done and who's going to do it.

2) Eliminate wet or slippery surfaces

It's really all about traction. Traction control procedures should be constantly monitored for their effectiveness. Keep all floors free of moisture. Use adhesive striping material or anti-skid paint whenever possible, as well as moisture-absorbent mats. Make sure they have non-slide backing material on them.

3) Clear all obstacles in aisles and walkways

Injuries can also result from trips caused by obstacles, clutter, materials and equipment in aisles, corridors, entranceways and stairwells. Put policies or procedures in place for keeping the area clean and clutter free. Also, avoid stringing cords, cables or air hoses across hallways or in any designated aisle.

4) Create and maintain proper lighting

Poor lighting in the workplace has long been associated with an increase in accidents. Keep work areas well lit and clean.

5) Wear proper shoes

Improper shoes, or those worn down, have the ability to cause trips, slips and falls. Whenever a fall-related injury is investigated, the footwear needs to be evaluated to see if it contributed to the incident.

Your employees are the backbone of your Club—and on the front lines of creating a positive member experience. They also face the greatest risks, whether working in food service, landscaping, or making sure the lights never go out. It's your job to protect your employees from on-the-job injuries, to the best of your abilities. This will in turn decrease disability, medical and workers' compensation costs.

Action Points:

- Qualify candidates for physically demanding jobs

- Create a injury management process and partner with your occupational doctor

- Identify your hazardous jobs and train to prevent injuries

A Final Thought:

"If we have honest conversations about what's working and what isn't, we can become really good. If we don't, we never really help each other." - Dave Barram

Chapter 11

Protecting Your Team

"There is NO substitute for WORK."- Vince Lombardi

The 2020 NBA season was deemed a success because the players were able to isolate themselves inside what was pretty much a hermetically sealed social bubble. They existed in one hotel and played in one arena; with strict limitations on who could enter. It was a safe haven in a COVID world.

Unfortunately, Private Clubs—short of dropping a plastic dome over the entire property—can't live in such a utopian world. Thus, a Club is vulnerable to the dangers of both the inside world *and* the outside world. Dangers that could result in annoying minor fines or something so egregious it threatens to shut your Club down. But this doesn't mean protections can't be put into place. They can and they should.

When you come onboard as a new GM, there is some information you should immediately track down; who are my managers and supervisors, who below them are the influencers among the other employees, and who is protecting me from the outside looking in?

What you want to have in place is a seasoned medical professional familiar with your Club and the duties your employees perform, an attorney willing to eat their young to prevent a lawsuit from taking your Club down, and a Risk Manager who can mitigate any small problem from getting big and big problems from getting bigger. To put it into football parlance, this protective triumvirate is your equivalent of the Pittsburgh Steelers' "Steel Curtain," the L.A. Rams' "Fearsome Foursome," and the Minnesota Vikings' "Purple People Eaters."

Let's look at the three components separately.

When it comes to choosing a medical professional, it's important that they have a healthy understanding of what the job entails so they can determine, should such an event arise, what the injured worker is capable of doing when it comes to planning a return-to-work scenario. To that end they should take a tour of the Club and, conversely, it's a good idea to take a walk through of their facility. After all, this is the person you are trusting with the well-being of your most valuable commodity; your employees. Doctors need to understand and see all the different jobs that you have, plus how you expect your injured employees to be treated. But you also need to set a certain level of expectations as far as communication goes. So if somebody goes in to be treated, you are being brought up to date on what they can lift, push and pull.

Injured employees need to believe they are being treated by the best doctors available, not just an occupational physician who they may perceive has in mind the best interests of the Club above their own. You are flirting with danger if you've had 10 people complain about the level of medical service they received. Because that's when the injured employee starts Googling *"Injury Lawyers."*

Your doctors have to be part of your strategic team so they can flag things when they arise. You want them to have a keen eye should there be a reasonable suspicion that an injured employee isn't what he says he is, or not telling the truth about what his on-the-job duties entail. And conversely, you need to make sure the clinic you are using is doing the proper testing as well. Think of it as a circle of trust. Because while all this is happening there could be decisions being made on whether or not to terminate someone, which can open up a can of legal worms. I believe for the most part claims can be avoided if you take your time and ask the right people the right questions. And, just as important; get their feedback. Do you have the documentation? Do you have the necessary write-ups for when you will be doing this? Is the employee in a protected class? Let's face it, you are being guided down a rocky path that could be a legal minefield, and at the end of the day all this due diligence may not be a silver bullet, but it will go a long way in protecting your Club.

Speaking of attorneys, despite what William Shakespeare had to say about them, they are a valuable team member. Still, it's imperative that this person be a specialist when it comes to serving your needs. You don't want to enlist a "generalist," someone who specializes in everything from divorce proceedings to trusts & wills. You want this person to be laser-focused on the potential dangers to your Club, someone who has intimate knowledge of your policies and procedures as well as your employee handbook, and will run with them. An attorney that will constantly provide you with legal updates so you know what is coming down the road before you get hit by a lawsuit the size of a tractor trailer. Someone who is intricately aware of how big you are, where you are located, and how many employees you have? Because if they don't have this information when something does happen it's like going to the ER and they don't have any of your medical records. If the attorney you hire is still preparing for a fight that you're already in the middle of, it's like going into battle with one arm tied behind your back. You shouldn't be shopping for an attorney when you have a claim. You want someone you have confidence in.

For instance, depending on the severity of a claim, sometimes I may have my $850 an hour attorney, sometimes my $600 attorney, and sometimes my $350 attorney on the case. So I say to a Club, tell me how bad it is. What are we looking at here? And who's representing them? If it's the attorney with the purple Lamborghini, I say let's go with the $850 attorney because I can tell this guy we're going up against is The Hulk in a courtroom. But if the employee found his attorney on TV advertising 1-800-Sue-Me, then I'll go for the lower priced attorney because you're likely dealing with a shyster. If you pick the wrong attorney, the claim could be going on for years with billable hours and all the stress, anguish, and depositions that accompany it. And all the while you are thinking, "We could have saved time, money, and stress by taking the right route with a specialist."

Here's a good example, we work with one attorney and he's $850 an hour and worth every penny. You want the claim to be over and done with as quickly as possible, and for that you need to bring out the executioner. His fee may seem high but what's the ROI if your Club gets hit with a multi-million dollar settlement? He's not friendly. He's not fun. But all the judges respect him, all the other plaintiff attorneys fear him. What more could you ask for?

Which brings us to the third leg on what you hope is a very sturdy stool; your Risk Manager. And short of a 911 accident, very often this is the one person you will contact before the other two when things go south.

The Risk Manager is the person on your speed-dial when an employee is injured or HR wants to pull the trigger on some type of employment action, which is especially dicey in states like California where there are more protective leaves than leaves on a tree. A good Risk Manager is always on call when you have a situation because they will walk you through it, pointing out the good points and bad points, the advantages and pitfalls, because they are not emotionally involved. Their view is from 50,000-feet, so they can *unemotionally* tell you that they don't think you have enough to pull this particular trigger, and if you do it will look like retaliation. I tell my clients all the time that as a high-end private Club you have a giant bull's-eye on your back that makes both a plaintiff's attorney and the government salivate. You don't want to be another notch on either of those belts.

When it comes to selecting a Risk Manager you want somebody that knows you, someone you trust, and someone who will be in your corner if there is a claim, or an audit, or if OSHA comes knocking on your door.

Let us return momentarily to the subject of finding the right people. It's a pretty safe bet that any Club with thousands of members will find among their rolls very capable people who dabble in medicine, law and insurance. But when it comes to picking the right people, this is low-hanging fruit you definitely want to avoid (and thankfully some Club bylaws prevent working with members). Because once you open that Pandora's Box you'll find out that everybody's wife is an interior decorator and everybody's brother-in-law is in the construction business. See where this is going? What if you hire this person to build your clubhouse addition and they're over budget and delayed? Are you really going to sue a member? Talk about bad optics.

These people are your guardians of the gate, and just like your Head Chef and Director of Golf, you need to know that they're on your side and they're protecting you. Plus, they need to bring you up to speed on what has happened thus far; the good, the bad, and the ugly. You need to know if there has been a big class action lawsuit and everyone got a $5,000 check. You need to know if you had a close call with a union vote. You need to know if there is an issue with the taxes or payroll. And from a Risk Manager's side, you need a full understanding of your coverage. You need to know what to do if you were to be flooded, or have a fire, or have a golf bag full of new clubs stolen or a missing Rolex in a locker; what is your coverage? If you were to be down for four days with no power, what would it look like for business disruption? You need to be able to have an overview enough to say, "We have that covered."

You really need to have people on the team to be able to back you up, understand the contracts, be up-to-date on new laws and new regulations that seem to change like the weather, and to answer the questions that the members have, as well as your employees. This trio needs to be your advocate, for better or worse, holding your hand throughout the entire process.

It's very easy to have a situation blow up in your face with the financial well-being of the Club, which you've been entrusted with, suffering the collateral damage. But it can all be avoided—or at the very least mitigated—with a few quick conversations with some key trusted people who are watching your back.

Action Points:

- Who is your protection team at the Club
- Assess your current protection team
- Establish the absolute protection team

A Final Thought:

"Learn to see things from different perspectives. Never limit yourself to just one point of view." - Nargis Fakhri

CHAPTER 12

On The Goal Line

"If you want to WIN, do the ordinary things BETTER than anyone else does them, day in and day out." - Chuck Noll

You see it in football all the time, a player who has been on the team for 20-plus years, adored by the fans, active in the community. He was a star player in his day, making all the plays and winning accolade after accolade. But time is a fickle mistress and the years have caught up with this player. You try to give him something skillful to do; maybe punt coverage. But even that doesn't work. But you can't just cut him because of the potential blowback from his teammates and from the fans. So what do you do?

This is a dilemma many new GM's will face when they take over a Club. It's a pretty safe bet that there will be at least a handful of employees all 65-70-plus who have toiled for the Club since the Nixon Administration. But even though they are beloved by members, they are being challenged at some point because they can't do the physical things they need to do. But again, they know the Club, they know the members, they know everybody's favorite drink. Still, it's not unreasonable that you just want people to actually be able to do their jobs. But part of the problem is they haven't been transitioned and put in the right position for them to succeed.

As we mentioned in the last chapter, we live in a society where lawsuits come at the drop of a hat, which means many GM's shy away from asking questions like, "Are you still able to do this job? Is there anything else you would like to do?" But they are completely justified in asking it. It's like having a caring, empathetic, and compassionate conversation with a family member, although that person could take it the wrong way.

Perhaps the problem is you are asking a question without giving a possible solution, like, "Can you help onboard new team members and tell them about the Club? Why don't you mentor our future leaders? Can you help us document the best practices and procedures in your department? Would you like us to look at other opportunities that would require less strenuous physical work? Can you be our brand ambassador and help us teach others about our Club culture?" You're going to have some very loyal veteran employees and they're not going to want a lot of change. In fact, some have made the Club their first and ONLY job. And part of that push back is their fear of the unknown; of what lies out there once they no longer have the Club as a safe haven? And I can't stress enough; everyone is going to be looking at how you treat people that are a little bit older.

The issue I see is a lot of Clubs never prepare their employees for retirement, that they never give them the financial education to prepare them, or even have a discussion in regards to next steps. Think of it as a paternal responsibility, like trying to explain to an elder parent what a 401k program is. Most people have it, but have little or no understanding of what it is or what it does. Bring in an outside financial expert to sit down with the employee and show them exactly what they have and what it means to them going forward.

Education needs to be available to all, not just those in the 65-plus club. In fact, if the staff feels that they're being pushed out the next thing you know there's a workers' comp claim looming on the horizon, or maybe a discrimination claim or an age discrimination claim. And any employee who goes out on workers' comp at 65 isn't likely to bounce back as fast as someone who is 22. So that claim is going to cost somewhere in the neighborhood of 3-5 times more, because a regular slip and fall may turn into the need for surgery, rehab, medication and lifetime limitations.

The key is to identify the right team members and the job that fits what they can do physically and mentally and that they actually enjoy the work. I ask Clubs to look at the player and determine if they are ready for a game or could we be putting them in harm's way?

If you have 30% of your employees that are 62 or older, you can't shy away from the obvious fact that some of these jobs are mentally and physically very challenging. Do you have people in place to transition them to less taxing duties?

There are three particular points that are very important for people to retire successfully. First, I think it's the need to understand their **401k** or retirement program and make sure they know what they're looking at. Should they be aggressive? Should they be more conservative? Is that really a hardship loan that they should be taking out? Second, do they understand **Social Security**? And the third part is **Medicare**. You need to have those three pieces in place as they are very important to succession planning. If your veteran employees don't know if they are going to have health insurance, they will never leave.

And if they're not quite sure how much they're going to get from Social Security, they may never retire.

I have one Club I work with that has bilingual retirement planning education. They bring in a professional who talks about how your 401k account is like your garden. And she asks what a mutual fund is? What is a bond? And depending on your age, what should your garden look like? Should we be really aggressive with tulips and roses? If your employees have never been taught about 401k's and what they mean, then you have a paternal responsibility to give them that education so they can retire with respect. Explain to them that when they go on Social Security they automatically get Medicare A and eventually Medicare B. But make it easy to understand. A lot of advice is given online and they think the best way to communicate with older folks is simply to use a bigger font. And once it's explained clearly and precisely, you'd be surprised how many people say, "I never knew that." It also pays to know as much about your employees as possible. I tell managers and supervisors they should know where their workers want to be in three years to five years. What are their hobbies? You should know their likes and their dislikes. If you have a very good relationship, make it part of the fabric of that annual review to ask, "How are things going?" Keeping a pulse on your department and individual team members is critical for planning, budgeting and forecasting.

If you ask, "What are your plans?" you'd be surprised that by having an open-ended conversation you might find out a lot about a person. Some will come out and say, "I'm gone in two years." Some may say, "I'm going to die here (and some do)." Others may say, "I'm moving to be with family." Having that information is valuable for a manager and for their department to plan and hopefully recruit from within or externally.

Give your veteran employees the tools to understand their 401k. Because as much as you want employees to be physically healthy, you also want to make sure that they're financially healthy as well. The last thing a Club wants is to have somebody retire and pass away a week later. Give them the tools they need so they can go on to the next stage of their life. This can be done with education outreach. You may also want to look at creating a retirement program. The criteria could be based on years of service and because they've been so loyal the Club would reward them with a package. In fact, right now due to risk factors it just makes sense for both the Club and the employees to look at a retirement option. Because, once again, everyone's watching to see how you're treating your loyal veterans.

What I see is that when the veterans are able to have some sort of connection with the Club, they come back to the holiday parties to see old friends. They come back for the big member guest tournament to be an ambassador that embraces the traditions of the Club. They are part of the culture of the Club. They're the fabric of the Club. And members love that. It's part of that memorable and amazing member experience. It's the person that was in the locker room when they were growing up, and the maitre d' that remembers what table you always like to sit at. And I think it's wonderful for the Club because it reinforces a sense of family. We believe in the member experience. That's when employees understand your mindset: "You dedicated your life to bringing smiles and happiness and creating great memories, and we're not going to kick you out. We're not IBM or Xerox where all you get is a gold watch and off you go. No, we're going to keep you a part of the fabric of our Club."

Trust me; if you do this all of the other employees will think to themselves, "Wow, I can actually come back and be part of the fabric of the Club, even when I decide to retire."

Action Points:

- Create financial education for team members

- Create a succession plan for your veteran employees

- Create a continual connection with your loyal team members

A Final Thought:

"The best leaders will be those that listen to their people to figure out where they should be going." - Jack Kahl

CHAPTER 13

Super Bowl MVP

"A CHAMPION is simply someone who did NOT give up when they wanted to."- Tom Landry

It's extremely rare that the player chosen as the Super Bowl MVP is some practice squad guy who barely plays. No, the overwhelming choice is usually a player who has displayed the same skill set throughout the season that he displayed in that key game. That player—for 16 games—used their vision, dedication, commitment, blood, sweat, and tears to make their Club the best there is.

For an entire season you've eluded dangerous pitfalls and protected your team's blind side. You've been the leader people have looked up to, even if some of the incumbent staff were non-believers; you won them over and you should be proud. You made sure you had the right players in the right positions, comfortable in the knowledge that they could get the job done. And you were proven right. They bought into your vision and the Club is better for it. You created an unbreakable circle of trust that led to this great victory. And along with a great team, you were well-protected by an inner circle that included your attorney, your risk manager, and your team physician. They were there guiding you from pre-season to the big game, while at the same time helping to reinforce your vision.

You sent accolades to people who were doing a great job, rewarding and thanking them for their efforts. But at the same time you kept a wary eye on who's on the injury list, who are the naysayers, and who are the prima donnas. And although you kept your eye on them, you never hesitated to stay positive, to let the Debbie Downers know that despite their trepidations they were always welcome to join you on the journey; all they had to do was hop on board.

Now you can sit in your office, look out the window, and feel good in the realization that you are not only the best Club, but also the *desired* Club. Maybe there's even a waiting list to join because members know you and your staff are rock stars, and you've created a love-fest between members and employees.

You're having fun, right? You had to go up against people pointing out how they've always had it like this for 30 years. The status quo. And to your credit you showed them there *was* a better way to do things. But they weren't just changes for the sake of change. You made *your* vision *their* vision. And the Club reaped the benefits of everyone being on the same page—the same playbook.

Congratulations! But remember; there's always another season ahead.

Action Points:

- Look at your vision
- See how your vision was executed
- Thank those that made the vision a reality

A Final Thought:

"If people believe in the company they work for, they pour their hearts into making it better." - Howard Schultz, Starbucks

59230007R00076